Pacts With
The Devil

"The Devil"
Part of a Set of Tarot Trumps Painted by S. Jason Black

FRONTISPIECE

Pacts With The Devil

A Chronicle of Sex, Blasphemy & Liberation

by
S. Jason Black
&
Christopher S. Hyatt, Ph. D.

Illustrations by
S. Jason Black

THE *Original* FALCON PRESS
TEMPE, ARIZONA, U.S.A.

International Standard Book Number: 978-1-935150-26-8

First Edition 1993
Second Edition 1997
Third Printing 2002
Fourth Printing 2009

Illustrated by S. Jason Black
Cover Art by P. Emerson Williams

The paper used in this publication meets the minimum requirements of the American National Standard for Permanence of Paper for Printed Library Materials Z39.48-1984

Address all inquiries to:
THE ORIGINAL FALCON PRESS
1753 East Broadway Road #101-277
Tempe, AZ 85282 U.S.A.

(or)
PO Box 3540
Silver Springs, NV 89429 U.S.A.

website: http://www.originalfalcon.com
email: info@originalfalcon.com

I cling unto the burning Aethyr like Lucifer that fell through the Abyss, and by the fury of his flight kindled the air.

And I am Belial, for having seen the Rose upon thy breast, I have denied God.

And I am Satan! I am Satan! I am cast out upon a burning crag! And the sea boils about the desolation thereof. And already the vultures gather, and feast upon my flesh.

Yea! Before thee all the most holy is profane, O thou desolator of shrines! O thou falsifier of the oracles of truth! Ever as I went, hath it been thus. The truth of the profane was the falsehood of the Neophyte, and the truth of the Neophyte was the falsehood of the Zelator! Again and again the fortress must be battered down! Again and again the pylon must be overthrown! Again and again must the gods be desecrated!

— Aleister Crowley
The Vision and the Voice

Lucifuge Rofocale
Prime Minister Of Hell

Based upon a seventieth century illustration in the
original *Grand Grimoire*.

TABLE OF CONTENTS

Part II
Practice

Appendices & Poscripts

INTRODUCTION

And the Lord God said, behold, the man is become as one of us, to know good and evil: and now, lest he put forth his hand, and take also of the tree of life, and eat, and live for ever:

Therefore the Lord God sent him forth from the garden of Eden, to till the ground from whence he was taken.

So he drove out the man; and he placed at the east of the garden of Eden Cherubims, and a flaming sword which turned every way, to keep the way of the tree of life.
— Genesis 3:22-24

To write a book such as this in today's repressive environment is either an act of courage or stupidity. We do not know which. Yet, we have a sense of what our "folly" represents. From the point of view of reputation it may be an act of stupidity, but from the point of view of liberating mankind from slavery it may be an act of courage.

The problem of evil is an ancient one. It would be simple to invert the meanings of good and evil and let our work rest on that worn-out maneuver. We will not do this. Instead, like our adversaries, we shall assert that the struggle between good and evil is simply a struggle about the role of man in the universe. Is man "free" or is he property?

Man has almost always been property to one degree or another. A piece of property can be used by its owner, sold, leased or rented. A *free* man cannot be treated that way, unless, of course, he consents. A *free* man can take his own life. A *free* man can ingest what he wills and live as he sees fit. He can choose to help another or not. If he chooses to live with others, we assert that he must obey one rule: not to initiate violence to get what he wants. Thus evil, if such a term is needed, is simply, for us, the initiation of violence. This is, of course, what the government and the church do to you if you disobey, since they have acquired a monopoly on "legitimate" violence. Thus, though we promised not to invert the classical meanings of good and evil, we inadvertently have.

An important quality of evil—as it is commonly under-stood—is that people are hurt. This fact can not be helped. To give up being a "free" man in order not to be hurt is no guarantee that "bad things will not happen." Besides, it is the act of a coward.

Every modern government makes a "social contract"—a pact[1]—without, of course, the consent of the populace—that it will protect and care for its citizens if they give up their right to care for themselves. Each government has certain sectors of human life which "belong" to it and things which do not. Government has taken for itself the monopoly on initiatory violence. For example, you can own property as long as you pay taxes. This is "ownership" based on the contingency of obedience. Thus, in one sense, *no one* owns property. The government provides for taking your property—by force if necessary—if you don't pay your taxes by claiming that you have violated the social contract (i.e., "the common good.") This refusal to obey by a magical act of metaphysics is transformed into the "right" to do violence.

To promote the idea of a social contract, something other than overt power has to be invoked to make the contract absolute and inviolate rather than simply arbitrary. This

---

[1] It is important to remember that a person becomes part of the pact (the social contract) simply by being born at a particular place and time. Thus, as with many things, the accidents of birth determine to a large extent a person's future. Further, it is fascinating to think that the most important deals one makes are made without one's consent.

power is usually God, or in the case of America, "the will of the people" together with their vision of God. Thus, for men to accept their status as property, a metaphysical assertion is needed. Some principal is required which can both stir and terrify people. Also, a history is necessary to legitimize keeping people as property. Each government or church has its particular wonder stories which are fed to children when their critical faculties are weak. At the base of all "evil empires" is the ability to inflict punishment. Without it the slave would be less inclined to obey.

To refuse the services of the politician, the priest, or the psychiatrist is an insult—to them. To negotiate for yourself, to be your own priest, your own psychiatrist, your own politician, is sacrilege, insanity or criminality. What label they apply to you is a function of who has the most power as well as the accident of who apprehends you first.

In our "free" (as long as you obey) society, each mediator—politician, psychiatrist and priest—are in competition. But they also cooperate in a larger sense to assure that society—their power structure—is being served. Regardless of which of the three is deciding what to do with you for violating the prevailing "customs" of normalcy, *someone is deciding for you*. You are an object that is being processed. You are not a real person, but simply a function—a piece of property. Most people rarely experience this because *as long as you don't violate the rules of society your real status as property is not invoked*. Yet, deep within each of us, we are aware of how little it takes to come to the attention of the authorities. Once they focus on you, your status as property is revealed and you are *processed*—thus revealing your status as: non-person.

Before the reader thinks that this is a book about politics, let us say that politics addresses the issue of whether or not you are property or a "free" man. The area on which this book focuses is the realm of the spiritual. Are you the property of some God or are you a "free" man?

In the spiritual realm there are owners, keepers and shepherds of men—as well as friends. The latter include those groups of spirits—at least in myth—who are relatively friendly toward man and want him to have more power.

The Promethean myth is but one example of a God-force that wants man to be intelligent instead of ignorant. Prometheus' "father" (Zeus), on the other hand, wants to keep man ignorant—a simple slave.

Prometheus is the divine rebel—a "Satan" who commits god-like crimes against the patriarchy. This is the critical point: that Prometheus, like Satan, is not man's enemy but is the enemy of the authoritarian tyrant whose desire is to rule man.

A similar myth is repeated in the Garden of Eden story. The Serpent (often called Satan) tempts Eve to eat from the Tree of Knowledge and become God-like. In some quarters Eve's temptation is seen as an initiation by the serpent Nechesh whose number is 358. Coincidentally, this is also the number of Messiach (Messiah).

The idea of preventing man from becoming a God is nowhere better exposed than by the Gods themselves when they decided to refuse man access to the Tree of Life. Genesis 3:22 says, "And the Lord God said, behold, man is become as one of us to know good and evil: and now, lest he put forth his hand, and take also of the Tree of Life, and eat, and live forever." In Genesis 3:23 and 3:24, "Therefore the Lord God sent him forth from the Garden of Eden, to till the ground from whence he was taken, so he drove out the man; and he placed at the east of the Garden of Eden, Cherubims, and a flaming sword which turned everyway to keep the way of the Tree of Life."

The Christian-Judeo religion system views man as property. The evil-one, the tempter is seen as a force which "makes" man disobey his master. The evil-one tells man not to obey his master, but to follow his own will. This, too, is folly since most men do not have a "will."

Disobedience, as well as pride (independence), are the two fundamental sins of the "evil-one." In fact, sin in the religious as well as the secular context is simply *disobedience*—the refusal to be a slave.

As children we are taught by our parents to obey, most often without question. The attitude of obedience is so deeply implanted by the time the child is seven that the "arguments" against his being a free man are well sown. In many instances, children and adults will argue against their own freedom. When the child reaches adolescence any rebellion against its early training is seen by adults as dangerous and disrespectful. Most adolescents retire from their rebellious behavior by the time they reach their mid-20's. Their "wild oats" have been sown and they begin to take their place in society as adults. By the time their children are born they have a full blown case of amnesia about their own childhood feelings and experiences. Now, as parents themselves, they inculcate their children with the beliefs and attitudes they learned when they were brainwashed. Although some changes are made by each generation, the primary attitude of obedience and conformity remain intact. Family tradition, religion and allegiance to a particular master are implanted into each generation. Each adult acts as if his particular programming is unique to him and somehow superior to other people's brainwashing.

THE PROBLEM OF GOOD

The problem of evil can not exist without the problem of good.

How can *good* be a problem? Simply by making it dependent upon the existence of evil. Yes, if good means obedience to religious and political paternalism, and evil means rebellion against these oppressive forces, then:

To see evil as a problem is to see good as a problem.

In other more common terms:

Good for most of us is simply the lack of evil.
Evil for most of us is simply the lack of good.

Or is it?

Both good and evil are concepts of the human mind. As concepts they appear opposed to each other—or so it seems.

However, to say that good and evil are concepts in no way limits the possibility that we interpret non-human forces operating in the universe as good and evil—from our human perspective. But because we label these forces as good and evil doesn't mean that they *are*—in some *absolute* sense—good or evil.

While we prefer to believe in the existence of non-human forces we have no "proof" of their existence in the scientific sense. More, we have no proof that these forces *are* good or evil—or that even our human concepts apply to them.

What we do have proof of is how humans label their own experiences.

To conceptualize events and experiences as good or evil is simply a function of what disturbs us and what doesn't. Thus, good and evil are simply a function of pain and pleasure. Yet as concepts they appear to have an independent status.

To understand the world in terms of good and evil is simple. To believe in the independent existence of good or evil—in terms of what pleases or displeases us—is nonsense. If good and evil exist independently of our understanding of them, we can have no idea about what these terms mean.

To generalize our personal experience to the impersonal—or the transpersonal—plane is the act of either a genius or a fool.

If everything were easy, if we obtained everything we wanted, then we could easily believe in the goodness of the universe. If we are frustrated or hurt we might believe the universe evil. Both feelings appear to be necessary and both are lies.

The issue is simple: *good and evil are human inventions which humans treat as non-human realities.* Thus, there is a confusion about the hierarchy of the concept. It is similar to Kant's *positing* an unknowable world beyond reason and then later acting as if it really existed.

When good and evil are attributed to otherworldliness—which by definition can't be known—we simply humanize the spiritual world. To use terms which we have assigned to this other-world and then act as if these terms didn't originate from the world we *do* know is one of our greatest errors. *If* there is another world we can only know how it effects our particular nervous system. We can't know if the effects of another world are good or evil except through our lenses.

If there is another world it can only be known through our methods of knowing. It can't be known by us "for what it is" through other methods of knowing.

To speak of Gods and Devils and Demons as good or evil is simply a statement of our reactions to what we believe their expressions or existences are for us.

THE PROBLEM OF EVIL
THE PROBLEM OF SUFFERING

To be confused by suffering is to be confused by life. Those who are confused by suffering require a meaning independent of their existence.

Suffering is human. The body is soft, the world is hard. To invent explanations about suffering is simply a narcotic.

Each explanation assumes something about the nature of life—it presupposes an "ought to" which is simply—"I want."

To assume that the world was—or can be—idyllic is to wish for slavery. To say *no* to suffering—to improve your life—is simply a desire. It is not a given.

In fact the Garden of Eden story indicates man's "suffering" over *not* suffering. To want to know, to be curious, is the nature of man—to want to control—to want immortality on his own terms—to create stories—this is all the nature of man. Curiosity is the curse of man because, according to the Garden of Eden story, curiosity and willfulness finally brings expulsion from paradise. To be curious is to disobey. Curiosity is the fundamental characteristic of all newborns. Yet, for whatever reason, curiosity is also associated with danger—and with evil. Did you ever notice that humans become less and less curious as they become older? The reason is not simply age. The "will to curiosity" has been beaten out of them. "It is better to follow the path of the tried and true." In this sentence the word "better" means "safer."

To try to explain suffering as purposeful or otherworldly is a sign of a weak stomach—and an over-active brain. Suffering is motivation to put "an end to it" for a while. Without struggle man is no longer man.

To live in the Garden of Eden is simply a death wish—which, if ever achieved, would put an end to the species known as man. Curiosity and rebellion are the basis of being human. Yet we are taught to obey. We are taught that there is a correct way to live—ordained in another world and enforced in this one.

Many men make an issue out of their suffering. Insurance policies are inventions of those who know how much humans desire to control suffering. But to be without the potential for suffering is to be without life. To make a life out of one's suffering—or for that matter one's joys—is folly. Unless you have a lot of talent.

There is no way out of life—until you are out of it.

Some invent, others endure, some go mad. Sometimes it is difficult to tell the difference.

Suffering is the foundation of creativity. To suffer well is a sign of an extraordinary human being.

To enlist spirits to put an end to suffering—or to give you what you want—is an act affirming man's desire to have power over his condition.

Whether a particular moral "philosophy" labels a spirit as good or evil, the attempt to *evoke* is a leap beyond rationality and science.

To say that Satan or the devil is responsible for man's misery is simply a matter of preference. One can just as well call God evil and Satan good. This frequent reversal of common morality is no more proof of good and evil than the common way of viewing things.

Each person must decide, if they can, what spirits or gods serve his particular desires and destiny and, if they be so inclined, ally themselves with them.

All spirits desire physicality. Each wants something, whether its name is Yahweh or Lucifer. Yahweh demands obedience and Lucifer appears to want to annoy Yahweh.

To *trade* with a spirit to get what you want is, in our view, more manly and often more sensible than praying for what you want.

There is a significant difference between praying and trading. During begging, impossible promises are made. Often these promises take the shape of being "good" in character or deed. Thus the typical prayer consists of a "sacrifice" of an "evil" quality in order to obtain something else. Usually people are incapable of giving up their vice in order to obtain the graces of God.

In trading there is an exchange of something tangible for something tangible. The person wants something and the spirit wants something. They make a deal. This type of exchange is often what makes the pact evil in the eyes of religious people. The idea of trading with God or demons is abhorrent to people, but this is exactly what people do when they pray. The differences seem to be of attitude and practicality. In praying a person begs. In a magical pact the person trades, bribes, threatens and commands.

Trades with spirits are commonly seen as an exchange of the soul for something tangible. More often than not spirits are not interested in souls. As some writers have said, Satan already "has" their souls. Spirits, like humans, want applause, praise and attention. For example, some people promise certain demons temples, or books written about them or dedicated to them. In fact some have charged us with writing this book to pay off certain spirits.

Spirits want visibility, while humans want powers and special favors. Thus theirs is a dynamic relationship between spirits and man. They are continually in process.

ABOUT THIS BOOK

The original title of this book was *Le Dragon Rouge* (The Red Dragon). While this book was not intended to be that original work, we felt the original title conveyed the power and force which this book shares. As we were finishing this work, however, we learned that Herman Slater of The Magickal Childe in New York was publishing the original book titled *Le Dragon Rouge*; thus we decided to rename our work so as not to confuse it with the original. (Mr. Slater died shortly before the appearance of this book. We will miss him.)

Since the fundamental character of this book is that of Pact Making with the Devil suggested to us to change the name to *Pacts With The Devil*. While not as romantic as *Le Dragon Rouge,* it does convey the contents of this work rather well.

Though this book provides historical information, it is not a book of history. Though it presents psychological information, it is not simply a book about psychology. It is a manual, written by two individuals with very different backgrounds, who have agreed on a fundamental issue: that pacts with the Devil are not as uncommon as some people would like to believe.

Many people—including those involved in the occult— do not believe that pacts or rituals or evocations or invocations "work." We have observed that most people do not actually *perform* ritual—they just talk about it—and therefore the claim "it does not work" is spurious. And more, the rituals that most people *do* perform are rather formalistic and dry.

The idea of the *pact* or *deal* is as ancient as man himself. How many deals with people, forces or God(s) does an average person make in his lifetime? This is difficult to know but we do know one thing—all humans make promises, all humans negotiate and the heart of negotiation is an exchange of something for something.

Unlike other animals, humans and "gods" make and break promises. It is fascinating that making a deal or a promise carries the assumption that one has the power to deliver. Thus, every deal is act of pride and every promise is a potential lie.

To believe that one can deliver implies that one believes—or hopes—that the world is orderly enough to allow for prediction and control. In this sense every promise is by definition a lie. Thus, the notion of Satan as a liar is true, but its truth lies in the notion of "truth" itself.

No one can control all the known, let alone the unknown, forces which can affect a promise. This reality is so obvious but so infrequently stated that law books are filled with contingency plans and penalties when a promise cannot be met because of one set of circumstances or another. Obviously, to break a promise because it simply does not suit you is frowned upon. Yet, people do this every day, finding excuses or reasons so they will not bear the consequences of their actions. Lawyers make a very good living penalizing people who agree on one thing and do another. Indeed, all currency systems are based on a "promise" to pay.

Promises, pacts, deals and covenants all rest on faith and hope. All children brought up in the Christian-Judeo tradition have dabbled with promising God. Even those who claim to be atheists make deals with forces. Pacts and deals are made in almost every relationship imaginable. Faith in promises is like faith in grammar. Everyone uses it but nobody knows what it means.

Regardless of who one is promising, a promise is always a seduction. It is a *sexual act*. Thus the notion of promise in itself is evil, is Satanic, is a pact with the Devil. No man can guarantee the future and few men have enough "virtue" or cash to pay for all the broken promises they have made.

Self-delusion is self-blindness. It is from this ability to delude that man builds theories and ideas which have no function but to create hope. There is no one who doesn't live on hope. Everyone is a "hope addict."

The average man makes promises which are often the most bold aspects of his character "…to love, honor…until death do us part." How noble, foolish or rigid must one be to believe such hogwash? How can someone with the body of an ape think so much of himself to make a promise? Is not the pride of the promise the essence of Satanic pride? Yet, we all make promises.

When I promise to Lucifer, I promise to someone who at least has an interest in my getting what I want. Conversely, the shepherd and keeper are concerned with my getting what they think I should have.

For man to say *no* to the "keeper and the shepherd" is a victory in and of itself. IHVH (Jehovah) and the fictionalized Jesus are the "keeper" and the "shepherd" respectively. Yet, the "true" stories about Jesus say that he was a rebel.

To say *no* to our fictionalized Gods is to say *no* to submission. It is not a *yes* to ego and a *no* to what is beyond ego. It is a statement of "I will not beg nor will I submit, but I will trade." The Pact with the Devil is a symbol of a freer man in a freer market place who has a sense of "equality" with his makers. It is an honest trade. To see man trying to influence the universe to his benefit, honestly and openly, well, that is the sign of the Promethean spirit. Is this the God-man that so many intellectuals have been speaking of?

Lucifer is more the Greek Prometheus than the Christian Satan. Thus, a pact with Lucifer-now-Satan—he who is loathed by the keepers and the shepherds and their slaves— is man contracting with a friend: Prometheus-Lucifer-Satan.

To make a pact with the Devil or any spirit is to negotiate for yourself. This is *true evil*—according to the church and society. Recall that Jesus rebelled against both. You have rejected their help, their intermediaries, and most importantly, their authority. This is the ultimate evil—the crux of sin—to disobey—to refuse the services of those in power— to deny their authority over your life.

It is often said that the sins of pride, egotism and disobedience are the sins of the Devil. If this means that ego is the *sole* creator then we have ignorance, not sin. The refusal to be grateful—to worship a creator—has to do with the ability to tolerate fear. Recall the old saying: "no one is an atheist in a foxhole." I hope no one believes that this proves the existence of God. I believe it simply shows what man is capable of when he is frightened.

Pacts with spirits require work and effort and should not be done frivolously. Often it is easier to use conventional means to get what you want. However, after these means have been exhausted, a pact will provide you with a sense of power over feelings of helplessness and the frequent desire to simply submit to the circumstances of life.

To know whether a pact can work for you is a question of experimentation. The experiment alone can give you a new sense of yourself. In fact making a pact with a spirit may allow you to observe how your mind works. It will also give you an opportunity to break free from some of the conditioning and brainwashing of childhood. At worst it will help you change your point of view. At best it may bring you what you desire.

— Christopher S. Hyatt, Ph.D.

A Note On The Frontispiece

The picture is that of "The Devil", part of a set of Tarot trumps painted by myself.

He is presented as a Dionysian/Promethean figure of great beauty and (to Judeo-Christian culture) threatening sexuality. His apparel is black and red, the colors of the *Macumba* deity *Eshu*. The open third eye of illumination is pictured on his throne and on the demonic image behind him, which imitates the images of liberated attainment as seen in Tantrik iconography. The trident—symbol of both the Devil and Shiva—leans behind his throne. At his feet are two of the uninitiated, enslaved by fear, addiction, misconception and habit.

The male cleric is a deliberate cartoon of the Irish Bishop who was recently disgraced for giving hundreds of thousands in Church money to cover up an illegitimate child he fathered.

I thought he was nearly the ideal of the type that I meant.

— S. Jason Black

PART I

HISTORY

CHAPTER ONE

The Foundations

The book that you are holding in your hands represents a corpus of literature that forms the very heart of the European esoteric tradition.

In the last twenty-five years or so, books on "magic" have concentrated largely on Kabbalism, Jungian psychology or the "neo-paganism" of so-called "Wicca." But for the three centuries following the Renaissance, the serious practice of magical art consisted essentially of the kind of systems collected in this book.

This material represents what is normally considered "black magic," since the spirits it pretends to consort with are admittedly demons. It is also, as we intend to show, transcendental magic, since the practitioner places his very soul and mind on the line (in traditional belief at least) in order to become more than a man: To achieve the power of a Magus.

While these rituals may be based on original manuscripts that were slightly older, the three Grimoires collected and adapted in Part II—*The Grimorium Verum*, *The Grand Grimoire* and *The Constitution of Honorius*—first saw some kind of general distribution between the end of the seventeenth century in France, during the twilight of the reign of Louis XIV, and the middle of the century following.

While the Church triumphed over the religious hermeticists of the renaissance, it can hardly be said to have eliminated the practice of sorcery, or for that matter, to have even slowed it down.

The "white" magicians such as Giordano Bruno or John Dee who openly advocated magic were seen by people of similar interests and talents to have martyred themselves for nothing. They gave their lives trying to win over individuals and institutions which were their sworn enemies (a fate modern parapsychologists might do well to take note of). So while their more idealistic colleagues either languished in prison or were barbecued in the city square, the more clandestine and cynical variety of practitioner simply kept a low profile and applied for protection to the officialdom of Hell. After all, events had proved who their friends really were.

THE ARISTOCRACY OF BLACK MAGIC

In spite of its status as a Catholic country, and probably because of a series of kings that were rather lenient on the matter (or like Henri III, active practitioners of magic), France was the spot in Europe that proved the most fertile and safe ground for the professional magicians.

These people escaped the witch burnings of the period for two reasons: first, the principle victims of the witch trials were the peasantry of Lutheran and Calvinist countries. Contrary to historical myth, the Inquisition was far less destructive of human life than were the new Protestant sects. And second, the people who formed this underground were more or less educated people who were protected by their clients, the aristocracy. Sometimes they were themselves aristocrats. This is a topic rarely mentioned in orthodox history books, but a number of people quite prominent in the political life of Europe were active and committed adepts of ritual magic.

One famous example was the notorious Francis Hepburn, "the Wizard Earl" of Bothwell, who consistently used black magic both to aid his political career and to eliminate, or attempt to eliminate his enemies. He was also a friend and client of the sinister "Doctor" Simon Forman, who was, if contemporary testimony is any evidence, one of the most gifted psychics, not to mention amoral practitioners, of his age.

The question, of course, that is central to anyone interested in this field of endeavor is: does it work? The answer that most people on the street would give of course, is "no," but that is nothing more than what we are programmed to believe by our culture (our inquisition, you see, has become internalized).

People like Bothwell, and others who will be mentioned later, had the same concerns as any modern prime minister or general. They were also the finest minds and most powerful personalities of their time and would be no more likely to repeatedly waste time with things that didn't work than any modern military strategist. Many of these people kept magicians on retainer throughout their careers, and to call them superstitious is merely begging the question. Also, many of the personal accounts of magical practice and its alleged results—like the Simon Forman material— are entirely consonant with modern studies of psychic phenomena, although coming from people using completely different concepts and frames of reference.

THE DIABOLICAL DUKE

The particular rituals we have here probably date from about a century before the French Revolution. Louis XIV was recovering from a series of disastrous and bankrupting military campaigns, giving free rein to the nobility and people of the court. It is difficult for a person living in our century to comprehend the kind of privilege and personal power into which the upper classes were born.

Versailles was a vortex of intrigue, corruption and sex (of all varieties). People who lived in this stressful and competitive atmosphere used whatever tools they could find not only to further themselves, but just to survive. Tools like coercion, seduction, blackmail, poison—and black magic.

At the top of the pyramid of these "predatory" personalities was Phillippe, Duc D'Orleans, nephew of the King and one of the people in line for the throne of France. He was brilliant, literate, amoral, literally murderous if crossed, an active bisexual and, since his youth, a practicing adept of the black arts. In the words of his Uncle, the King, he was "a walking advertisement for every type of vice and crime." This man was a member of a number of secret societies that existed at court and in Paris. He may have been introduced to them by his father, the King's brother, nicknamed "Monsieur," a committed homosexual who stopped buggering his pageboys long enough to create heirs to the Dukedom and who was known to charge into battle on horseback with a sword in one hand and an open parasol in the other.

Apparently Phillippe's interest in black magic began at an early age, and he became one of the central figures in a secret network of magicians, alchemists, poisoners and pimps that extended from the highest ranks of the French nobility to the criminal underworld of Paris. To call this man a genuine Satanist would be no great exaggeration. Born to power, he clearly considered himself "beyond good and evil" and in modern terms would probably be labeled a sociopath. For example, he had an incestuous relationship with his daughter up until the time of her marriage. Apparently, when the honeymoon was over, he saw no reason for her married state to keep him from his pleasure and visited her on a regular basis in order to bestow his Fatherly affections upon her.

Eventually her new husband got wind of the relationship and was understandably upset. To smooth things over, the Duc invited his son-in-law to dinner. Sometime between soup and dessert the man became violently ill and died in his bed a few days later. This is how the Duc earned the nickname "Phillippe the Poisoner." There is considerable suspicion by historians that he was personally responsible for the death of the Dauphin, grandson of Louis, thus paving the way for him to become Regent of France after the King's death.

That one of the rulers of the most powerful country in Europe was a multiple murderer who spent many of his nights offering the blood of goats to the Devil sounds like the most lurid kind of fiction, but it is historical fact disputed by few. This is the world in which the rituals in the second part of this book were born.

While it may seem that the "black arts" were at their darkest at this period, it should be mentioned that the aforementioned Simon Foreman was also famous as a healer, and the magical and hermetic books of the time were one of the major influences on Isaac Newton.

CHAPTER TWO

Possible Origins

THE HELLISH PRIESTHOOD

Another major part of this occult underworld was the clergy. Anyone familiar with the history of Christianity, both ancient and modern, is aware that it is an amazingly legalistic faith. You "accept Jesus as your saviour" or you are "baptized" so that you become a recipient of God's "grace" and you are assured a place in Heaven no matter what kind of a miscreant you are.

Conversely, if you are not a Christian you will burn in Hell forever, however brilliant, kind and talented you may be. This, of course, is a simplification, but not much of one.

The French priesthood at this time contained an enormous class of impoverished and mostly out-of-work priests and "abbes" that were far too numerous to find a real place in the functioning hierarchy of the Church. In one sense they were leeches, yet in another they can be considered victims. Sons of the peasantry were sent into the Church to get the education and living that their fathers could not provide, as well as second sons of the aristocracy were given to the Church because they would not inherit— or simply to get them out of the way.

These people were fully trained in the rituals of the Church, but many of them had no parish from which to make a living. They supplemented their meager incomes and fended off starvation by selling their services. By services, we mean they would accept money for saying "masses" for the benefit of the payee. This included seduction, the gaining of wealth and even murder.

From the point of view of a seventeenth or eighteenth century priest there was nothing particularly contradictory about such actions. They were baptized priests. They had been given the power by the Church, which had been given the power by God, and nothing prevented them from using the power as they saw fit—especially if it provided dinner. The mass was viewed as a magical act that had power *in and of itself* regardless of the purpose for which it was performed. This practice became so common, and was taken so seriously, that at least one priest was executed during this period for accepting payment in order to say a funeral mass in the name of someone's (still living) husband. The goal of course was his death.

Not all of the activities were murderous, however. A certain Madame de Lusignan was caught with her priest, frolicking naked in a forest and practicing "abominations" with an Easter candle.

While the majority of these characters confined their activities to more or less orthodox Church rituals, there were a certain percentage who "crossed over the line" into the practice of diabolism and black magic. They conjured demons, created talismans for clients, and performed the famous and semi-legendary "black mass." This is where the legend comes from that it is necessary to be an apostate priest in order to perform a black mass. In those days there was no dearth of apostate priests.

It will be noted by readers that the *Constitution of Honorius* in the later part of this book is written to be performed by a Catholic priest and the book implies that it was written by an initiate of the Church itself, under the direction of the Pope.

A.E. Waite, in his *Book of Ceremonial Magic,* ridicules this idea in his usual incoherent fashion, but he makes it clear that his attitude is only the result of his own relent-

lessly middle-class religious ideas. In fact, leaving aside the
clearly fictional participation of a Pope, we find nothing
more likely than that this book was written by a renegade
priest. The author's understanding of the function and
design of ritual is sophisticated and elegant and the
assumption of the power of the Catholic liturgy says
"priest" to us in a way the other two rituals included in this
book do not.

DARK GODS OF AFRICA

One more suggestion should be made regarding the
authorship of all three of the rituals collected here. During
the period when they first appeared, the colony of Haiti,
then called San Domingue, was the richest possession of
France. Though this is not the place to go into a history of
the subject, most people are aware of the unbelievable
brutality that was demonstrated toward the imported black
slaves by their Christian masters, who where brought to the
island literally in the millions.

While the practice of African religion was outlawed by
the overlords of the island, the population of slaves was so
huge that they could not be prevented from practicing some
things in secret. During the time of the French possession,
it seems almost certain that a number of Europeans took an
interest in, and learned from, the imported beliefs that later
became Voodoo. The whites, after all, formed intimate
relations with their slaves, thus creating the large mulatto
class on the island. It seems likely that some of these
relationships became close enough that the whites were
taught a little, or perhaps a great deal, of the African ritual
tradition and translated it into their own terms.

The reason why this kind of influence seems more likely
with these three books than other manuals of black magic is
because of their structure. The classic Grimoires do not
contain full rituals. Books like the *Lemegeton* and the *Key
of Solomon* contain lists of spirits and talismans, along with
conjurations and threats to be repeated by the sorcerer until

results occur or he dies of *ennui,* whichever comes first. The three rituals we have here all begin with extended purification and sacrifice, as well as the ritual creation of the proper tools. In the case of *The Constitution of Honorius*, this process extends over the period of a month. This exactly parallels Afro-Caribbean magical processes practiced in every major city in the Western hemisphere. (Santeria alone is estimated to have a following of five million in the United States.)

In these rituals there is repeated cleansing of the celebrant, various animal sacrifices, the creation and empowerment of sacred weapons, culminating in the evocation of the spirit. The only difference is that in the Afro-Caribbean practice, this results in the physical possession of one of the celebrants. European magic (including modern "Wicca") avoids this natural and historically universal experience as a result of the Judeo-Christian fear and hatred of the supernatural. As a result of this complex structure and commitment of time by the magician, these rituals amount to systems of self-initiation, as well as extended meditations with a distinctly Tantrik flavor.

APOSTATE NOBILITY

We have implied earlier that this kind of magic was, during this period, largely the province of the upper classes. We will give two examples of the practice of diabolical magic among the rich and powerful—personages who almost certainly owned, and probably used, the three Grimoires in the second part of this book.

While we have said that the atmosphere in France was rather more lenient than elsewhere, sorcery was still illegal, and the magician clumsy enough to place himself in the attention of the authorities could still go to the stake. (According to some sources, the last *official* burning for witchcraft took place in Poland in the 1790's.) In the case that has become known as "the affair of the poisons," the death and imprisonment of a network of hundreds of practitioners began, as so often, with *someone's big mouth.*

In our remarks about the Duc D'Orleans we said that he was associated with an enormous secret network of black magicians and other bohemian types who existed at court and in the environs of Paris. In the late 1670's this underworld was (temporarily) exposed to the light of public scrutiny—with a vengeance.

A foreshadowing of these events occurred in 1668, when a fortune-teller named Le Sage and a priest named Mariette were arrested by the civil authorities and charged with sorcery. According to the court testimony, the two men made their principal profits by the manufacture of love charms which the priest then "charged" by placing them underneath the chalice at mass. This was hardly unusual, but the court got a shock when they were given the names of the sorcerer's regular clients, all residents at Versailles, all high nobility, including the mistress of the King and the daughter of the judge.

The evidence and testimony was immediately suppressed and instead of death, Le Sage was sent to the galleys and the priest was banished for nine years. After only a short stay in the galleys, Le Sage was released by one of his powerful clients and returned to Paris to continue his "work."

Jumping forward a decade in time, a dinner party was given at the home of a successful Paris dressmaker, and as the evening progressed, the guests become more than a little drunk. One of the guests, a woman named Marie Bosse, was a professional fortune-teller and remarked— probably in a slurred voice—"What a lovely occupation is mine! What classy clients! Nothing lower than duchesses, marquises, princes and lords. Three more poisonings and I retire, my fortune made!"

Unfortunately, one of the people who overheard the remark was a lawyer who was a friend of La Reynie, the King's Lieutenant-General of police. The wife of one of La Reynie's officers was sent "undercover" to investigate, and on the second visit to the fortuneteller, she was offered poison to be rid of a fictional unwanted husband. She duly reported these events and soon after the police were breaking down the door. The Bosse woman was apparently caught in a sexual situation with her two sons and her daughter. The wife of the aforesaid dressmaker was also arrested.

Further investigation (including the use of torture) led to a woman nicknamed La Voisin (real name, Catherine Monvoisin). Not coincidentally, she was the mistress of the sorcerer Le Sage, who we have already met. Shortly after the arrest of La Voisin, Le Sage himself was arrested once again, and for reasons of his own (Francis King has suggested intense jealousy of La Voisin, but an hour on the rack is just as plausible) told the police everything they wanted to know.

DEMONIC UNDERWORLD

La Voisin was the organizer of a Mafia-like group of sorcerers, alchemists and renegade priests who had garnered a fortune by performing black magic and compounding poisons for wealthy clients.

Imagine, if you will, the scene when the authorities took possession of the various residences belonging to the members of this group: the police arresting the occupants and proceeding, perhaps, to a cellar or loft and finding altars with candles made from baby fat, circles drawn on floors used for demonic invocation, fully equipped chemical and alchemical laboratories with racks of toxic herbs for the making of poisons. In addition, organic substances used in magic: powdered blood and sperm; skin, hair and body parts; and semi-precious stones to make talismans.

There were libraries of every available tome on the practice of magic (including, possibly, the ones in this book, which one of these people might even have authored). And a large stove in the workroom of La Voisin contained the half-incinerated fragments of human children. All in all, a scene worthy of a Hammer film.

It must be said that most of the remains discovered in La Voisin's oven and elsewhere were the remains of abortions, another of this enterprising woman's businesses. Nevertheless, she and her colleagues were guilty of the ritual murder of infants on several occasions.

Once the full extent of the criminal conspiracy and the possible number of murders became known, La Reynie got permission from the King to form what became known—for rather obvious reasons—as "the burning court." This was a tribunal given special powers, by order of the King, to interrogate persons of noble rank (who would otherwise be immune to such a subpoena) and to mete out penalties to the guilty. By the time this court was finished, more than three hundred people would by imprisoned, banished, or burned at the stake for the crimes of murder and sorcery. This, by the way, was a civil court, not an ecclesiastic one. The work of the court came to an end, not because it was finished, but because people of such high rank were implicated that just as he had personally authorized the court to begin with, the King personally ordered it disbanded and much of the evidence destroyed.

THE MALEVOLENT MISTRESS

The King's action was due to the involvement of his mistress, the Marquise De Montespan, his lover of many years and the mother of several of his children. Her involvement started when she came to believe that the King was losing interest in her. True or not, she was worried enough to engage the services of La Voisin to make love philters which she introduced into the King's food. According to the testimony, these love potions, like so much of what these people did for their clients, seemed to work, and the Marquise was satisfied. But eventually the King's roving eye began to worry her again, on top of which she seems to have developed an ambition to be made Queen.

For this kind of problem, stronger magic was needed and La Voisin brought in her principal partner, a priest named Guiborg. If this man had been invented for a novel, the author would be criticized for stretching the credibility of the reader. In his late sixties, at the time of his arrest, he had apparently spent his entire life in the practice of depravity, vice and sacrilege. Described in the court records as a libertine, he boasted that for at least the previous twenty years, he had made a profession of the saying of the black mass on the bodies of women, and had sacrificed "countless" children at these altars.

It would be comforting to believe this man a lunatic and some kind of pathology is certainly evident, but the police had good reason to believe he told the truth. When his services were acquired by Madame Montespan, he arranged to perform a number of black masses, usually upon the body of La Voisin's daughter. He would read a liturgy dedicated to "Asmodeus and Astaroth" rub the (presumably stolen) consecrated host in the girl's vagina, have intercourse with her and sacrifice an animal or bird whose blood was drained in the chalice and mixed with the host. This mixture was dried to powder and mixed with the King's food.

Whatever the events that followed, the Marquise remained dissatisfied, and two more black masses were performed, at one of which she seems to have suffered herself to be the altar, and at both of which the throat of a small child was cut over the chalice as the offering. While the entire diabolic liturgy has not survived, there is a fragment in the court records which gives some idea of the style and atmosphere of the ceremonies. At the moment of the offering, Guiborg supposedly recited:

> Astaroth and Asmodeus, princes of fellowship, I invoke you to accept the oblation of this child for that which I ask (on her behalf for whom this mass is celebrated): that the King and the Dauphin will continue their friendship toward her, that she will be honored by the princes and princesses of the royal family, that the King will deny nothing she asks of him for her relations or household.

When the Sun King, who saw himself as nearly divine, discovered that his lover had for years subjected him to the manipulations of witchcraft and been a participant in child murder, he must have given a new definition to rage. Rather than suffer the humiliation of having this known, he stopped the proceedings at once, sealed the evidence and—need it be said—ended his relationship with the Marquise De Montespan.

La Voisin went to the stake, hundreds of others were imprisoned or banished, Guiborg died in a dungeon and for a little while, the demons were left in peace by the citizens of Paris.

CHAPTER THREE

Heirs To The Tradition

HELLFIRE DASHWOOD

While the power of the Church remained strong amongst the middle and lower classes and still retained the ability to punish transgressors, the upper classes freed themselves more with each generation. By the beginning of the eighteenth century, an educated person could express a certain cynicism toward religion and the bible without much fear of punishment. There were exceptions to this. Rome was certainly one, so was Spain, both of which had active inquisitions until the arrival of Napoleon.

In England and on the continent, groups of wealthy young men formed clubs specifically for the celebration of blasphemy and diabolism. Some of these were serious, and involved the practice of the Black Mass in its various forms and even demonic evocation. Many were overblown frameworks for the defiance of authority and sexual indulgence. The principal practitioner—if that is the appropriate term— of this era was Sir Francis Dashwood, Baronet.

Dashwood seems almost the archetype of the eighteenth century rakehell. Accounts, both real and probably legendary, date from his early twenties describing him as a man of violent passions who took delight in vice and blasphemy and who, like the Duc D'Orleans, seems to have been a conscious Satanist.

One famous story will serve as an example: during the 17th and 18th centuries, until the Napoleonic wars made such travel impossible, there was a rite of passage called the Grand Tour. This was where young men and (less frequently) women of the upper classes would be supplied with money to take a year or two to travel around Europe. This was generally done after finishing their formal education to equip them to live in "society." Depending on the character of the travelers, it could also mean several years of uninterrupted partying. Dashwood, like other young men of his class, went on this Grand Tour and seemed to take particular delight in his stay in Rome. There were several reasons for this. First, it was the repository of some of the great art collections of the world and also, like Paris, a place where one could obtain forbidden books and learn about unusual practices.

During his stay in Rome he did as tourists do to this day: he attended a service at the Sistine chapel. It was Good Friday and some sort of ritual scourging was involved in the ceremony. Presumably it was night, because the chapel was in darkness. When the (very light) scourging began, Dashwood, who was in the congregation, pulled a bullwhip from the inside of his greatcoat and started thrashing people left and right, whooping like a banshee. He was forcibly ejected from the chapel, and subsequently from Italy.

THE BROTHERS OF ST. FRANCIS

When he returned home, carrying with him the books and experiences collected on his travels, he began to live the life expected of a man of his class—which at that time was a combination of politics and debauch. His personal indulgences soon took a rather dark turn. Around 1745 or 1750 (opinions vary on the date) Dashwood "officially" founded the Order of the Friars of Medmenham, the satirical name of an organization devoted to the more structured practice of activities Dashwood had been obsessed with throughout his life.

The "rites" of the Friars of Medmenham were celebrated in an abandoned Cistercian monastery located on an appropriately mist-shrouded island in the Thames. This Gothic ruin had been purchased by Dashwood and comfortably refurbished for this purpose. Again, there is some uncertainty as to the exact activities that went on there and later at the "hell-fire" caves dug into the chalk hills of West Wycombe. This is due largely to the destruction of the notes and financial documents of the Order by its secretary, Paul Whitehead, just before his death. Some writers assert that the members were out-and-out Satanists and others deny this, saying that Dashwood and his friends worshipped the goddess Venus. We suspect that both are true.

One of the things that Dashwood seems to have discovered during his sojourn on the continent was the pagan survivals, some of a blatantly sexual nature, that had been woven into Christianity, especially in Italy. This, combined with the study of the Grimoires which he apparently purchased on his travels, would have told him what the same study would tell someone today: that the traditions of black magic are the survivals of ancient beliefs and knowledge, and that Lucifer is none other than the Dionysus of the old world.

There is both a strong element of blasphemy and rebellion against Christian religion and also elements of pagan revelry in this tradition. The black mass, in its traditional form, is purely and simply an orthodox pagan ceremony in all of its components. It is not, as some "neo-pagans" like to claim, a branch of Christianity, but a pure survival that can be traced back to the mists of prehistory, just as the Christian mass has its roots in primitive ritual cannibalism.

At regular intervals, the "monks"—which always included twelve male celebrants plus Dashwood—would gather at the Dashwood estate for an extended stay. These included such luminaries as George Montagu, the Earl of Sandwich (yes, *that* one) and at least once Benjamin

Franklin himself, who had become a friend of Dashwood during his brief stay in England. The rest of the "regulars" consisted of poets, politicians and wits, some of whom could be considered the cream of their generation.

From London would come several carriages full of the most talented and attractive courtesans available, who would be lodged on the estate separately from the men in a "convent" under the supervision of an "abbess." Several days of preparation would ensue, with servants making sure the abbey was clean, warm and furnished and that there was enough food and—especially—wine. When night fell on the appointed day, the men would dress in monk's robes and the women in nun's habits (perhaps a little more revealing than the genuine article). They would proceed to the river and the waiting transport. This consisted of a large "raft" (probably what we would call a flatboat) lit by torches, which, when laden with its holy passengers, was rowed down the river to the abandoned abbey on its isolated island.

Exactly what happened next is, due to Mr. Whitehead's loyalty, a matter of some speculation. There was some sort of ceremony, possibly even a black mass. Here, the objections that the monks worshipped "Venus" *don't make much sense.* Why were the women dressed as nuns and the men as monks? They could all have worn togas if that was appropriate. (Roman revivalism was quite common at the time, especially in architecture.) But the symbolism they chose was largely diabolic, and inscribed over the entrance to the abbey, Dashwood had put Rabelais' dictum: "Do what you will." What is certain, is that after the ceremonial portion was over, the "nuns" were partnered with the "monks" for activities for which real monks and nuns would have to say a great many "Hail Marys."

The notion that the Medmenham *soirees* were more satanic than pagan is also supported by accounts of the decoration of the abbey. A man of enormous wealth and a connoisseur and collector of the arts, Dashwood had the taste, money and connections to furbish his temple in exactly the way he thought appropriate. The walls were painted with frescoes which have been described as "erotic" but were probably pornographic, and the altar was said to have painted caricatures of all twelve disciples. The workers and artists hired to carry out this project were all imported to avoid any gossip, and the abbey library contained an odd combination of pornography and theological works. The chapel itself was kept locked and was barred to all but initiates of the order. This secrecy was capped by the destruction of the order's papers, preventing us from ever knowing how far these people went in the worship of their deity. Could those papers have contained, perhaps, written pacts by the members pledging their allegiance to Lucifer?

CHAPTER FOUR

The Origin Of The Pact

FORBIDDEN ALLIANCES

The demonic pact was and remains one of the most anxiety-ridden subjects in the western esoteric tradition. There are two reasons for this that we can think of, and the subject shares these reasons in common with most psycho-spiritual practices that inspire automatic fear in our culture. Firstly, it lays the "soul" and "mind"—the inmost being of the practitioner—on the line. It commits that person to a contractual obligation with a metaphysical entity in return for services that would irrevocably change the magician's life. This is frightening because most people are terrified both by the thought of contact with a spiritual intelligence (which he may even claim not to believe in) and also by the thought of achieving his goals.

The second reason is that the conjuration of a demon and the creation of a formal alliance with it is quite possibly the oldest form of initiation known to man. It has exact parallels in every magical tradition in the world, both Christian and non-Christian (see the works of Carlos Castaneda for example) and goes so far back in time that our very cells acknowledge its power, even when we consciously "don't believe."

Let us emphasize here that despite the safari we have just made into the world of European "Satanism" and despite the use of the liturgy in *The Constitution of Honorius*, the material that follows in this book is *not religion* in the normal sense of the term. The manuals of magic collected here, especially the pact-workings, are the stuff from which religion comes (the covenant with Jehovah was a pact) and which modern religion imitates with empty formalism.

Someone once remarked to Jason Black that the definition of a religious ceremony is an act of ritual magic that doesn't work. The forces that are called up by these techniques, whatever the reader chooses to think they are, are communicated with directly by the magus and the practitioner must deal with this experience *alone*. This is the factor that everything in our Judeo-Christian upbringing tells us to avoid.

FAITH VERSUS KNOWLEDGE

In our culture, unlike, say, Tibet, we talk about *faith*, which has been sarcastically described as a belief in things one knows to be untrue. Direct experience—gnosis—is discouraged from every corner. This is true for the Jew, the Christian and the Atheist alike. If you don't believe this, we suggest you take a close look at the hysterical, almost panic-stricken way in which Psychic research has been attacked by all the above groups for strangely similar reasons, no matter how convincing the evidence or distinguished the researchers.

Even the religious convulsions of Pentecostals and their ilk are only encouraged *in* the group and to become *closer* to the group. These experiences—such as they are—reinforce programming. The goal of the practicing magus is to break programming and create himself anew by demolishing his previous limits. A person who breaks the limits imposed on him by the world at large is a very disturbing phenomenon. He doesn't respect authority and he makes a lousy servant. Religion prays to (begs) a hypothetical daddy figure for help and guidance. Magic *demands* communication and performance, or the being/force will be punished, or at the very least, ignored.

This kind of reaching out and treating with the unknown is the basis of much shamanic training. In those parts of the world where authentic shamanism still exists, the apprentice sorcerer is isolated somehow—usually by going into the wilderness—and calls upon the spirits to speak with him. Sometimes the conjuration involves the taking of psychoactive drugs, but not always. The fledgling sorcerer continues his efforts no matter how many days it takes to get a response. When the spirits come, the first thing that happens is usually an attack. The apprentice must defend himself. If he fails, this can literally result in death (whether from his belief or from other forces we will not speculate). If he succeeds, he returns to society with one or more *allies*, which aid him in the performance of magic. In return, he gives the spirit something that it wants or needs. This may be some kind of sacrifice, or even periodic possession of his body as a sort of temporary "incarnation." This is the story of Faust pure and simple, with the Christian neuroses about soul-eating removed. However, even this rather obvious ploy to insure the loyalty of Church-members through fear has primordial parallels.

GIVE-MAN

In Haitian Voodoo (and Voodoo is the only genuine "old religion" extant), there is a ceremony called the *Ba Moun* or "give-man" ceremony. This is performed by the *Bocor*, or professional sorcerer, as opposed to the *Houngan*, who serves the community. Whereas in the European tradition, the magus gives *his* soul in payment to the demon, in the Afro-Caribbean version, the person making the agreement can give other people's souls. This is believed to be a more satisfying arrangement. The catch to this is that he must give from his own family and friends. In other words, it must be a real sacrifice of someone he loves. Harsh as this sounds, if you think about it, you realize that this is far from uncommon in the pursuit of ordinary ambition. Say that a man is frustrated with his life. He has been honest and worked hard and gotten nowhere. He is at the end of his rope. He goes to the house of the *Bocor* and tells him these things, and in the way of such conversations from time immemorial, he says he would give "everything" to satisfy his desires.

So the *Bocor* calls upon the *Petro* family of spirits, which are very close to the concept of infernal demons, and the spirit speaks to the supplicant. He demands a written agreement signed in the man's blood, which is placed in a *govi*, or ritual jar, and tells the man that on a certain day, once a year, he must choose one of his loved ones to die as a sacrifice to the spirit. In return the spirit will satisfy all of the man's desires and ambitions. If this is agreed to, one person a year will mysteriously sicken and die to satisfy the spirit until the day comes when there is either no one left that the man can give, or he can no longer bear to commit such an act. This time the bargainer himself is taken. It is an eerie coincidence that one of the *Petro* spirits that operate these pact agreements is called *Bosu Tricorne*—the three-horned god. Look at the illustration of *Lucifuge Rofocale*, the infernal maker of pacts at the beginning of this book and you will see what we mean. Perhaps the lord *Lucifuge* spread his activities further afield than France. Or perhaps our earlier suggestion that a former resident of colonial Haiti wrote *The Grand Grimoire* deserves some consideration.

ARCHAIC ROOTS

Whatever the ultimate origins of the Grimoires of Part II, the tradition of the pact with "the Devil" goes back to the early dark ages in Europe, when the Roman empire was falling apart in earnest and Christianity, which had been the state religion of Rome for more than a century, was in conflict with the older beliefs of the people.

At that time, some of the then-existing histories were transformed by Christian scribes to accommodate the Jesus myth. A good example of this is Merlin, who, according to the research of Nikolai Tolstoy (in his book *Quest For Merlin*), was a historical figure who lived during the fifth century AD in one of the still-pagan enclaves of northern Britain. He is considered to have been the last great pagan prophet of Europe and thus a figure of considerable importance.

Christian chroniclers, however, have transformed him from the last of the Druids into a half-human figure whose father was a demon (or the Devil himself). In typical fashion they make him one of the great knowledge-givers and guides of Western legend and simultaneously damn him to hell for his magic.

In this same way, the pact-working was cut off from its ultimate roots in prehistoric magic (while still retaining most of its essentials), to become the dangerous selling of one's soul to everlasting hellfire, for the privilege of exercising supernatural power on Earth.

Possibly the oldest of these legends deals with a Churchman of the name Theophilus. Theophilus was a humble scholar who enjoyed the quiet and safety of the monastic life. Unfortunately, his reliability and talents attracted the attention of his superiors in the Church, and he was offered the recently vacated office of Bishop. Pleading humility, he refused, which proved to be a very bad move. The office was given to the second choice, an ambitious politico who proceeded to torment Theophilus at every opportunity. He made his life, so to speak, hell. This state of affairs continued, until Theophilus was finally fed up, at which time he took a forbidden book from the monastery, and in a crypt in the wee hours, called up the Evil One.

The Devil told Theophilus that, in exchange for his immortal soul, he would give him the power to do wonders and triumph over his enemy. Theophilus, at his wits end, agreed. Events went as Satan promised, and the Bishop met his demise. In due course, Theophilus was offered the Bishopric a second time and this time accepted. Years passed, and his power and reputation grew apace, but as he grew older, fear began to gnaw at him. He thought more and more on death and even though he knew that he had served the Church well, he also knew that when he died he would pass into Hell forever. He began to pray long hours in his private chapel, and his servants debated among themselves as to the nature of His Excellency's private grief. Eventually this whining attracted the attention of the Virgin Mary herself and she intervened personally on his behalf, forbidding the Devil his soul. *Deus ex machina.*

Aside from being an object lesson in the dangers of making a contract with an ecclesiastic, this little legend—which became very popular and much elaborated upon—contains all the ingredients that remain with us to this very day.

The scholar (religious or secular) who, driven to *extremis*, uses his knowledge to call up an evil spirit, sell his soul, and enjoy magical power. The performance of various wonders during his lifetime. The last minute regret for his actions which at the end, mean nothing to him. The self-castigation for his pride in disobeying Holy Mother Church. The inevitable descent into Hell (or in the case of Theophilus, last minute reprieve).

The first component of the myth goes back to shamanic practice. The rest is a Christian accretion to keep people in fear and bondage.

CHAPTER FIVE

Pacts In The Church

POPES OF SATAN

Theophilus was not the last official of the Church to be accused—rightly or wrongly—of being a black magician. Gerbert, Pope Sylvester II, who held office in the 11th Century, was a talented intellectual who acceded to the Throne of St. Peter when his native France and the Holy Roman Empire (in other words, the "civilized world") were in the throes of conflict. The role of the Pope in such a time was largely as some kind of peacemaker, using either diplomacy or direct threat. Considering the sort of person he is said to have been, it is entirely plausible that he may have practiced magic of one sort or another, but of course, the legend that grew up around him is much more lurid.

Gerbert, a native of France, was given to the Church by his father to get the education that his talent required and that he, a poor farmer, could not give. Gerbert thrived in the atmosphere of learning in the monastery, but there came a day when there was no more that these provincial monks could teach him. He was called to the chambers of the Abbot, and informed that he was being sent to the city of Toledo in Spain, there to act as secretary to the Bishop and also to pursue his higher education. The young monk was thunderstruck. Toledo was an open city where Saracens and Christians lived side by side and (shocking!) even Jews were allowed to practice their religion openly without persecution. He was frightened, but being an obedient son of the Church, he went. Thus far, the legend is probably historical fact.

In Toledo part of his "higher education" included mathematics, astrology and "natural philosophy"—the rudiments of magic. In the way of many country bumpkins suddenly exposed to the wider world, Gerbert slowly lost his fears and became more sophisticated. He began to explore the city and examine the merchandise and books that came there from Africa and the Orient. He also made acquaintances of a sort that he would never before have considered, among whom were Saracen practitioners of magic. It was from these that he eventually learned the art of calling up spirits and making them obey his will. Ultimately, he became ambitious, and setting his sights on the Papacy itself, he called up Lucifer and made a pact with him that he would be his minion if the Devil made him Pope. The Devil said yes, certainly, why not, but he must beware of one thing. He must never say mass in Jerusalem, because on the day he does that, his days on earth are over. Easy enough. The agreement is made, Gerbert becomes a master of the black arts and his career in the Church progresses at a "supernatural" pace.

Sooner than he would have believed possible—due to magically-aided deaths and promotions—he is created Pope. For years he lives the life of luxury and power that he longed for, until one day, on an official tour of some part of Europe, he says mass at the local cathedral, a church that he had never been in before. He is only part way through the liturgy when he notices that he is surrounded on all sides by demons. They are squatting on the gargoyles. They hang from the rafters. They fart at him from the choir loft. He realizes something has gone terribly wrong and, turning to the assisting priest (who sees none of this), asks what place he is in. He is told that this is the Church of Jerusalem. Gerbert knows now that he has been tricked and falls on his knees before the altar, publicly confessing all that he has done. It is too late. In agony, he dies on the spot and a coffin is prepared for his body and sent back to Rome. It was said that for years afterward, howls of pain and despair could be heard from his tomb in the dark of night as his soul was tortured eternally in Hell.

The truth of the above is (probably) that Sylvester II may have been a magician, but the diabolical aspects of his story were likely spread by his political enemies.

The second nigromantic Pope on our roster is the wonderful Roderigo Borgia, Pope Alexander VI. In this case the legends and the reality match each other very well. Father to Cesare Borgia and also to the notorious Lucrezia, this remarkable man exemplified both the light and dark sides of the Italian renaissance. We should make clear here to those unfamiliar with the history of the Catholic Church, that a person in the upper echelon of the Church hierarchy has only recently been expected to take the vows of a priest and work his way "up." Historically the nobility and people of power often entered the Church in what we would see as extremely unorthodox ways, and we are aware of one example (French) of a man who took the vows of priest on the same day he was made Archbishop.

Roderigo Borgia, was, like the rest of his family, a sensualist, an intellectual liberal and an unscrupulous master politician for whom the end justified the means. He was a bisexual, equally fond of his choirboys and his daughter Lucrezia (in common with the Duc D'Orleans), a patron of the arts, a libertine, and supporter of some of the major writers of the day. During his tenure as Pope, the so-called *Corpus Hermeticum* was translated into Latin for the first time and made available by the new process of printing. This became the centerpiece for the concept of *Priscia Theologia*, the "pristine religion."

The Hermetic texts pretended to be (and were believed to be) the writings of an Egyptian master of almost godlike genius and power, Hermes Trismegistus, thought to be the real person upon whom the Egyptian god Thoth was based. It was also defended by its proponents—who were many— as a pagan foreshadowing of Christianity and therefore to be considered as holy text alongside the Bible.

This caused some mixed feelings because, although the writings were very far from anything one would consider "black," they were nevertheless magical texts. During this time the principle exponent of this philosophy was Pico Della Mirandola, a priest and theurgist who was among the first to urge the Church toward a magical reform of its structure. For most people this is an unknown aspect of history, but the fact is, around the time of the beginning of the Protestant reformation, there were a group of thinkers within the Church who were urging a "Hermetic reformation"—a restructuring according to magical principals.

This movement saw its final failure when Giordano Bruno was burned at the stake in 1600 AD. While later Popes took an extremely negative stance toward magic as part of the Catholic counter-reformation, Alexander VI was liberal on the subject since he still felt secure. Martin Luther was still just a storm on the horizon. While it is by no means certain that he *practiced* magic, he certainly studied it, since he became one of the principle protectors of Pico, and had the hermetic texts included in the great Vatican library. He was also responsible for the decoration of certain rooms that he used in the Papal residence with frescoes (which still exist) depicting talismanic astrological images and an imaginary portrait of Hermes Trismegistus himself.

As we have mentioned, he is widely believed by historians to have had an incestuous relationship with Lucrezia— and with his son Cesare (who was also a cardinal!) The Vatican had an atmosphere that was neither sedate nor holy. With this in mind, it is no surprise that rumors of banquets degenerating into orgies and diabolical midnight conjurations became common in the rumor mill. For example, Alexander, Cesare and Lucrezia once had a contest in the Vatican where the contestants were the most beautiful prostitutes in Rome. They were stripped naked and went around the room picking nuts up off the floor. We leave it to the reader to imagine with what.

All of this was some centuries later than the life of Gerbert. Since the printing press had been invented we have first hand written accounts, rather than the wild stories that earlier times produced. But what is known to be fact is wild enough. In harmony with the classical revivalism then current, many of the public ceremonies performed in Rome at the time were openly pagan in content.

This was reflected in the way Alexander ran his Vatican. When Lucrezia was given in one of her many marriages, a drunken celebration was held at the Papal residence, and at one point, Alexander escorted his daughter to a balcony that overlooked an empty courtyard. Below them, a mare and an aroused stallion were led in by servants. Wine goblets in hand, the two laughed and watched the mare be mounted, His Holiness telling his daughter that this is what she should expect from her husband-to-be. Diabolical rituals may well have been held in the Vatican at the time of Alexander—certainly no politician of the time was averse to hedging his bets by the employment of magic. It is also significant that many of the major writers on magic of the time—Pico, Bruno, Ficino, Cardanus and Trithemius— were priests or monks, so the popular myths of satanic priests and prelates have a certain grounding in fact.

It is an ironic fact that Alexander was responsible for ordering one of the major European witch hunts. Witchcraft, as an opposing religion, was considered as a separate topic from magic at the time.

The last sorcerous Pope, of course, is Honorius III. Unfortunately, there is little to say about him except that he was given credit for *The Constitution of Honorius* which appears later in this book.

CHAPTER SIX

The Legacy Of Faust

THE DOCTOR & THE DEVIL

Of course, the figure central to all tales of pacts with demons is the one we have saved for last: Doctor Faustus. Once again, we have an admixture of myth and history, both of which provide some insights into our subject. As far as history goes, there seem to have been two "Doctors" of that name. One, the more shadowy figure, seems to have been a German Doctor of Philosophy in Wittenburg sometime before the year 1500. He is described in a few surviving pieces of correspondence as a practitioner and exponent of magic and a dangerous radical thinker. This, more or less, is all we know. If he wrote books, none have survived nor do we know when and how he died. What we do know seems to indicate that his status as a scholar was legitimate, and that his ideas (whatever they may have been) were taken seriously enough to cause official alarm.

The second Faustus we know far more about and what we know is far from flattering. During the lifetime of Trithemius, a charlatan called himself "George Faustus Junior" and proclaimed that he had doctorates in pyromancy and hydromancy among other rather odd degrees. This idiot lied and buggered his way across Germany and neighboring countries, using tricks like fireworks and magic lanterns to endear himself to the local merchant classes while sneaking his way into bed with their underage sons at night. Needless to say, he was frequently one step ahead of the law and almost certainly came to an unenviable end. Unfortunately, most of the popular stories about Faustus are based on the activities of this man. This is why one can see Faustus as the romantic ideal of the renaissance magus on one hand, and a subject for stories told by drunken 16th century inn patrons on the other. The latter was the chosen milieu of our friend "George," and many of the German folk-tales of Faustus may have been spread by the "Doctor" himself. In the folk-tales, as opposed to the dramas and poetry, Faustus is a vulgarian who is finally found dead in a gutter, done in by the Devil. This could be based on the actual death of "George Faustus Jr." who may have been done in by one of the men whose sons he diddled.

THE FAUSTIAN LEGEND

The myth of Faustus however is far more interesting and significant than the facts: After the Protestant reformation of Martin Luther, the social atmosphere in much of non-Catholic Europe became very anti-intellectual. We mentioned earlier that the Protestants were responsible for far more deaths in the witch trials than the Inquisition, and this is true. However most of the victims were lower class women, not at all the caliber of person that could be considered a magus.

However, there was now enormous pressure and scrutiny put upon the intellectual elite. The freedom of speculation that the renaissance had encouraged was beginning to be stifled with a vengeance. In Switzerland, the delightful John Calvin had Michael Meir burned at the stake for sorcery. His crime? He had discovered the circulatory system. Earlier, in Italy, the right-wing monk Savonarola had made pyres of "sinful" books and paintings, as well as people, robbing posterity of thousands of works by renaissance masters and crushing the creative spirit for a generation. During this time also, the educational system had changed radically, from a system of mental gymnastics that relied on memory exercises (what would now be called holism) and the use of the imagination (it was on this that Bruno based his magic) to the rote absorption of facts that we have today. This pressure, coming from Christian institutions on one side and some academic circles on the other, had proponents of the magical world view literally on the run.

On the continent, Cornelius Agrippa was hounded from city to city and country to country—now by Catholics, now by Protestants—because of his "Occult Philosophy." In England, John Dee, acknowledged as the finest mind of his generation, was robbed of a university position by his conservative enemies and died in poverty. Giordano Bruno died at the stake in Rome, a martyr for these practices. Under such conditions occult practice became a highly charged political issue and remained so until the 17th century. This was the time when the advocacy of magic began to go underground, ending up in the sort of underworld in which we found it during the reign of Louis XIV.

In this atmosphere, Dr. Faustus became a symbol of opposition, of protest against the sterile and materialistic direction in which things were going. He was, *at the same time*, the object lesson on what happens to the person who dabbles with things "man was not meant to know." He was the Agrippan magus, who dared assert, against the authority of the Church, his right to "mount to the heavens and unite with the archetype itself." He was the prince of black magicians who had abandoned all restraint and denied all authority over himself except nature, and nature he set out to master through magic. For the lower classes his life was the disastrous result of the dangers of too much learning, an attitude still held by modern fundamentalists.

Occult Literati

The job of distilling all of this was taken on by literature. First, Christopher Marlowe produced his *Doctor Faustus*, a drama that the late Francis Yates thought may have been a public attack on John Dee or Cornelius Agrippa. Here we have an aging Faustus, erudite and admired, but sick to death of respectability, who decides all that he knows is futile. He turns, almost sensuously, to his hidden cache of black magical texts, and declares his old affiliations over and his life as a conjurer begun. He conjures the demon Mephistopheles (the origin of whom is also a matter of much debate) and sells his soul for youth, knowledge and the satisfaction of all his desires. Not a bad deal. The point we want to make, that keeps the myth charged with meaning, is that from that time to this we are told *it's bad to want these things*!

It is this conflict between natural desire and Judeo-Christian repression that makes Faustus both a tragic figure and a Byronic hero. It is what saves him from being just another folk tale character like Gerbert. The Marlowe version sends Faustus to Hell in the end of course. Marlowe was an atheist and violently anti-clerical. His feelings seem to have extended to the field of magic. In spite of this, *Doctor Faustus* contains some of the most compelling and perceptive insights into the character in the whole corpus of the literature, especially in the character development of the first part of the play.

Two hundred years later, the other famous version of the story was begun by a young German named Goethe. This was a dramatic poem which the author continued to expand and revise until nearly the end of his life. The attitude displayed in this book is quite different, and reflects the changes that had taken place in the political and religious climate between Marlowe's time and his.

Goethe was a predecessor to the Romantic poets who would come a generation later, and his optimistic view of man's potential and lack of intimidation by religious authority shows throughout. In addition, Goethe was himself seriously interested in occult speculation, so his interest in the character was anything but satirical. Here also we find the aging Faustus in despair. His life is meaningless, his accomplishments worthless, he has decided to take his own life. Then he hears the church bells peal in the distance, and he is brought back to himself. He realizes, in a kind of satori, that there is more in the world to be explored, and he commits himself to the practice of magic, compromising his soul more in the fashion of a gambler making a bet than as an act of fatalism.

There follows an (extremely) lengthy series of wonders and sexual entanglements, far more complex than the Marlowe play. Goethe's ending however, is where the difference really shows. The anti-clerical of the 16th century sends Faustus to Hell, but the proto-romantic of the 18th shows the character as justified in his actions, and saved from damnation in the end.

As we said earlier, the pact legend is still with us. Most recently, popular legend has it that Fidel Castro won his revolution, not because of superior strategy, but because he had an alliance with the Seven African Powers of Santeria. In our country there was hot rumor for years that the rock band Led Zeppelin attained success through an agreement with the powers of darkness. And it is a fact that guitarist Jimmy Page is openly a student of the magician Aleister Crowley.

Having outlined the western European history and mythology surrounding pacts, it would be profitable to look at some parallels from other cultures.

CHAPTER SEVEN

Foreign Parallels

BLACK TRADITION OF THE EAST

The tradition that comes closest to the magical view of relations with demons is *Tantra.* Recently there has been a flurry of books published with the word "Tantra" somewhere in the title. Other than the translations of Hindu and Buddhist documents, almost all of these are trash. Of the many books written by American or British authors, only four we know of present the subject accurately and are worthwhile: *Aghora, At The Left Hand of God* by Robert Svoboda, *Secrets of Western Tantra* by Dr. Christopher S. Hyatt, *The Way of Action* by Francis King and *Tantrism, Its Secrets and Practices* by Benjamin Walker. We would recommend any of these to the serious student, as well as some works by Ajit Mookerjee and *The Rajneesh Bible* by Bhagwan Shree Rajneesh (Osho).

Most of the rest, including sexually explicit "how-to" manuals, are bowdlerized and whitewashed to the point where they are almost anti-Tantrik. The worst is a large and beautifully illustrated book called *Sexual Secrets* by Nik Douglas and illustrated by Penny Slinger. In our view this author is phobic about various forms of sexuality (most notably male homosexuality) and irresponsible in some of his medical assertions (for example: anal sex causes cancer). Be that as it may, his entire attitude goes against the grain of the *Vama Marg,* or "left-handed" Tantra that he supposedly writes about. The author seems to encourage the social bonding and compulsive relationship restrictions that Tantra seeks to dissolve. Upon the first reading of this enormous tome the thought came to mind that it should have been titled "Sex Yoga For Presbyterians." The pictures, however, are great.

BINARY FASCISM

The problem, not only with the above-mentioned work, but with the entire European approach to the subject is twofold: first, the twisted Judeo-Christian attitude toward sex has so narrowed our point of view that all many people see when they read about Tantra is sex. Tantra is "sex-yoga." While this is an aspect of it, it is only a tool—one of many. Second, almost all proponents of Tantra have been unable to face up to what it is in its pure form: the Left Hand Path, dreaded of Dion Fortune and turn-of-the-century Theosophists. In other words, the Western parallel is Goetic Theurgy—see *Aleister Crowley's Illustrated Goetia*, New Falcon, 1992—or demonic magic, the subject of this book. The attempt to force Tantrik philosophy and practice into a Christian's view of what is "good" or "positive" simply fails, because Tantrism, unlike Christianity, is not dualistic. Someone, even a "new-ager" or "occultist," who is born into the European Christian matrix will constantly be dividing things up into good and bad, positive and negative. How many of us know people who say, "I have a positive philosophy" or, "I only practice White Magic." They then point out a group or individual that they label "negative" and bludgeon them with their positive attitude. This is nothing more than Judeo-Christian legalism and judgmentalism in a thin disguise.

Jason Black once had a conversation with a "witch" in which she told him how she would never do anything "negative." She told him that "the Universe" had "chosen" her (her words) to serve it and, presumably, help save it from destruction. The conversation then shifted to her aversion to "negative" people. A positive person like herself just didn't like to be around negative people and *things always happened to them* if they kept their unwelcome negativity in her vicinity. Of course, she wasn't responsible for this mysterious punishment. It just happened. He has often wondered if this woman ever realized what she had told him about herself.

BREAKING THE FETTERS

Tantrism can be defined most basically as a body of psycho-spiritual technique whose goal is to free the aspirant from the bonds and limitations that social programming has laid upon him. This goal is the same in all forms of left-handed practice—whether it is Hindu, Buddhist, Taoist or Islamic. The complete fulfillment of the potentialities and goals of the aspirant is the *highest good.* This precisely parallels Agrippa's assertion that the goal of the magus is to "...mount to the heavens and unite with the archetype itself."

In practice, this entails the ritual desecration (deprogramming) of cultural taboos. In Bengali Tantra this takes the form of the "rite of the five m's" in which the Tantrika partakes of forbidden substances like beef, wine and drugs, and has sex with a woman (or sometimes a man or a boy) either not of his class, or forbidden in some other way. In European magic it takes the form of the Black Mass and the witch's sabbath.

The parallels are obvious and both traditions serve the same purpose in "freeing up" the psychic and emotional faculties of the magician.

A good example of this is the Hindu Aghori sect. These people are widely considered to be the most extreme practitioners of the *Vama Marg.* In *Aghora, At the Left Hand of God,* the author describes his guru's initiation as a young man. He was taken to a mountain village and instructed to do *japa*, ritual mantra repetition, sitting on the fresh corpse of a sixteen year old girl whose mouth had been filled with oil and a lit wick to make a lamp. In this macabre setting, he received his first vision of the goddess Tara, one of the terror deities of the Hindu pantheon. This goddess became his patroness throughout his life (note again the similarity to the pact commitment) and he even claimed to have been teleported to Calcutta as a result of the experience.

All of this—the necromancy, the evocation of embodiments of violent aspects of nature (which, be it remembered, are all considered to be people in the magical view), the ceremonies in graveyards—are all for the purpose of uniting the sorcerer with all parts of the universe. There is no division between "Heaven and Hell." Kali, the goddess of destruction, is looked on by Tantriks as a mother goddess. It must be said here that what has been described is part of the occult or esoteric aspect of Eastern religion, and is often viewed with shock by the orthodox. Nevertheless, in the Orient, this is a living, if underground, tradition. In our own culture it has been much more effectively killed.

TANTRA OF THE WEST

So in what way are the diabolical workings of these Grimoires valuable for a practitioner of our own day? We would say that they perform precisely the same functions as psychic tools for self-development as do the Bengali Tantrik practices or the Tibetan *Chod* rite and for the very same reasons. Why not then, simply practice Tantrik yoga? Because we cannot voluntarily jump from one world of mythic symbol to another without massive, often painful, change on a deep, irrational level and we have personally met very, very few who have even come close to doing this.

We know many people who have practiced Hatha yoga to great effect. This does not mean that the idea or symbol of a Hindu deity has the same impact on them that it would on a native Indian. For example, some identify the god Shiva with Lucifer/Satan. This is because his positive and negative aspects are nearly identical and because there is some evidence to support the idea that Shiva and Dionysus are the same god. (For example, we consider Dionysus to be the major archetype for Satan for reasons that will be stated later.)

All of this identification would hardly mean a thing to someone raised in the Hindu tradition because it is not a dualist religion, and Christianity is. No matter what we call ourselves, "neo-pagan" or "new age" or "yogi" or "atheist" we are still puppets for the patterns and fears etched into our minds with acid as a child. Unless we *directly* confront those symbols and fears, "principalities and powers," there will be no breaking free, and when that confrontation occurs, long-repressed forces will rise up that will result either in empowerment or collapse.

Twenty or so years ago, when the "Wicca" movement was still vital, Paul Huson produced *Mastering Witchcraft* (still in print). In it, he had a brief ritual of self-initiation where one renounced Christianity and said the Lord's Prayer backward. That was practically all it entailed. Most readers will be surprised to learn that Mr. Black personally observed that the practice of this simple, five-minute ritual created a major psychic upheaval in a noticeable percentage of the people who did it. They had panic attacks. They had nightmares. One even claimed to have poltergeist phenomena in his apartment. Those who were not scared off by the experience (and many were), and persevered in their practice, came out the other side feeling cleansed.

There were other changes as well. Some claimed to have become "psychic" where they were not before. Others had a feeling of freedom, or the ability to do things that they could not before. Many of these people also experienced profound emotional changes. Long repressed feelings of anger, hurt or even lust were released from the depths.

The sort of experience described above, is what *genuine* initiation produces. One such experience is rarely enough on any path of self-development, and the serious student would likely have to wrestle with these forces many times in his life, although it does become a bit easier with repeated experience.

CHAPTER EIGHT

Modern Influences — Fear & Repression

[The material in this section refers to S. Jason Black's personal experiences.]

Unfortunately, more than a decade of being active in and around long-standing esoteric groups has proven that ninety-nine percent of the participants will move heaven and earth to avoid such genuine results as those described at the end of the last chapter. Mr. Huson's ritual is no longer encouraged by any group I am personally acquainted with, and the once-promising "neo-pagan" movement has degenerated into a thinly-disguised Judeo-Christian religion that has ousted the horned god and goddess and replaced them with Jesus in a dress. One "magical" group that I have been involved with seems to have dropped the serious practice of magic in favor of empty religious rituals and stereotypical dead-guru worship.

About seven years ago, I was involved with a small group devoted to the serious use of the "Enochian System" of John Dee. Having discovered that I had talent as a trance medium, I became the principal "skryer" for the group, and practiced when I was at home alone as well. During one of these at-home sessions, sitting upright in an easy chair, I went spontaneously into a trance experience that I can only describe as orgasmic. Waves of ecstasy began at the bottoms of my feet and traveled slowly up my paralyzed body to the top of my head. This continued without letup for nearly half an hour with such intensity that I could hardly think. There was no stimulus for this but the magical practice itself, no drugs, no alcohol, nothing. I came back to myself feeling serene and elated in both body and mind and went to bed that night still feeling the same way.

I awoke the next morning instantly. That is, there was absolutely no progressive interval between sleep and full wakefulness. I felt the rushings from feet to head once again, but this time, instead of trancing out, I was filled with incredible physical energy. I began laughing spontaneously. The energy and joy continued to build as I prepared to go to work. My face was flushed and I continued to giggle periodically. (In fact, several people at work privately asked me if I was "on" something.) This condition continued unabated for *three days*.

I slowly realized what the reader may by now have guessed. I had experienced one of the more pleasant versions of a kundalini experience and I was anxious to tell someone about it.

I went down the street to the home of a friend in the Enochian group and found him in conversation with a group of his friends involved in "Wicca." *Good*, I thought, *I can get more feedback on my experience.* As I related my story, I soon realized that I was the only person there who had had such an experience. Not only that, but they were rather desperately fabricating reasons why this ecstatic experience was a "Bad Thing." I had lost control of the ritual, they said. I hadn't properly "earthed" the "energy" they said. I should come to their classes and they would teach me how to make sure such a thing would *never happen again.*

I was stunned. I had assumed that people who styled themselves "witches" would be as anxious to experience such a thing as I was, but what I encountered instead was an attitude of repression that amounted almost to an attack.

They had:

1. Established themselves as socially superior by asserting that my success was a "mistake."

2. Eliminated the need to face their own lack of results (failure).

3. Prevented me from becoming a competitive threat in their own social group. And:

4. Attempted to make me conform to their own limitations and to acknowledge their authority by urging me to join their "class."

All of this was a knee-jerk response that I have seen repeated a hundred times in different situations by different "esoteric" groups, of which the Wiccans are far from the worst. Trapped in a group like that, one might as well be in Church. The petty social dynamics are exactly the same.

SPIRITS OF THE AIR

By now it should be clear to the reader by now that I practice magic seriously, aside from just writing about it. I have found that most books on magic whose authors purport to be practitioners of one sort or another, quietly omit the relating of personal experiences and results. There is usually good reason for this.

Since the following pages deal with the issue of the conjuration of spirits and the idea of the pact, I feel obliged to state my position on the existence of such things. I will also relate a (very) few of the experiences that have led me to it.

It has become almost a matter of form for people writing on the modern practice of magic to flatly state that spirits are nothing but "parts of the human mind." There is currently a British founder of a "magical order" who, having shamelessly ripped-off Crowley, Austin Spare and Kenneth Grant, now states—on the basis of nothing—that spirits *come from* the "unconscious." This is drearily typical. Almost without exception these people have no knowledge of psychology, no knowledge of psychical research—especially as it relates to anthropology—and little practical experience. Also, almost without exception, they claim a belief in some form of afterlife or reincarnation. How this can work without an accompanying belief in spirits is unclear to me.

On the other hand, in a sense they can hardly be blamed. Since the end of the Renaissance, Western society has been under the domination of Calvinism and the Protestant world view—the direct parents of Victorian materialism—a fact often vehemently denied by the Victorian tradition. Nevertheless, historically, "God" became more distant from his creation. Psychic phenomena of all kinds were more and more repressed by the Lutheran/Calvinist influence. Ultimately, the witch trials stopped because there was no longer any need for them. The witches and sorcerers had lost their heritage.

To be sure, there have been resurgences. Spiritualism was one. So, in the view of some, is the UFO experience. You cannot wipe out something that is innate and perfectly natural to human experience. But it can be so smothered by ridicule, embarrassment and hostility that it goes underground. In other words, though people are still having the supernatural encounters that their ancestors had, either they don't tell anyone, or they transform the experience into something acceptable to their group—whether it's a UFO, or Jesus, or Jesus as the captain of a UFO.

Ironically, though not surprisingly, while the actual experience of a non-physical entity or spirit of the dead is *verboten*, pure superstition is not only acceptable but admired. Thus, if I proclaim my "faith" in "God" or take comfort that I will be in heaven with Granny and Jesus when "my time comes," I am assumed to be a wholesome citizen. Never mind that I may be a drooling ignoramus, my "faith" is harmless to the social order and keeps me pacified and obedient in this *best of all possible worlds*.

If, on the other hand, my dead father appears to me and twelve other witnesses and tells us the winning lottery numbers, and he's correct, we would be wise to keep quiet. Why? I suggest that you consider what the *fact* of life after death would do to the established authorities. Church, medicine and technology would be in a tizzy because this single fact would destroy more of their assumptions than I could begin to list. The linear causality belief of the man on the street would have to go. So when such a thing occurs— and it happens far more often than people suppose—there are only a few appropriate responses: You're a liar (ignore what you say). You're crazy ("put him on Thorazine"). You're a criminal ("we are going to prosecute you for fraud and put you in jail unless you confess").

Since people have a perfectly natural aversion to being thought silly, crazy, or criminal—or for that matter thinking it of themselves—magic has quite naturally become "pop psychology" or "meditation." Which, of course, from our point of view, much of it is.

This is definitely not to say that every evocation produces genuine contact with what seems to be an alien entity. Far from it. The majority of such experiences lay in a grey area rather like Jung's experience of "active imagination." This might be material from one's unconscious, or it might be "something else."

JUNG & THE ARCHETYPES

Since Jung was mentioned, we might as well examine his theory of the "collective unconscious." This has been used for decades by well-read occultists to justify both the operations of ceremonial magic and the idea that it is explained by psychology.

There is a subtle distinction between what Dr. Jung actually wrote when he formulated his idea and what it is popularly thought to be. The popular idea of his collective unconscious is that we all share similar "archetypes" and myth patterns in the depths of our minds that are somehow passed on through DNA. So, locked in our skulls, we share images of gods, dragons, fairies, etc. This idea is fine so far as it goes, but it is not what Carl Jung believed, according to his writing.

For Jung, the collective unconscious was something shared by everyone, but he did not believe it was bounded by any individual skull. That is, it was a metaphysical mind or space that interpenetrated everywhere, and could produce phenomena inside a person, *or in the outside physical world itself*, with equal ease. He also believed that this continuum contained knowledge of everything that has ever happened. In *Mysticism, Psychology & Oedipus* the Jungian analyst Dr. J. Marvin Spiegelman said of Jung's ideas in relation to magic:

> Jung had concluded that beyond the world of the psyche and its causal manifestations and relations in time and space there exists a trans-psychic reality (the collective unconscious), where both time and space are relativized. At that level there is acausality and space-time relativization parallel to the findings in physics.
>
> The archetypes are then conceived of as "psychoid," i.e., not exclusively psychic... This "psychoid archetype" is an unknowable factor which arranges both psychical and physical events in typical patterns... The psychoid archetype lies behind both psyche and matter and expresses itself typically in synchronistic events.
>
> Jung understood synchronicity as an acausal principle which stands behind such events as telepathy, clairvoyance, etc... Jung's conception of synchronicity is a great advance in the appreciation of occult phenomena and their linkage with both depth psychology and natural science. However, the peculiar experience of causality in the occult field, the sense that the magician can "will" or "produce" changes, seems not to be reached by this conception. Synchronicity helps explain the subjective experience, so important in life, of "meaningful coincidence."
>
> It also provides a hypothesis for understanding divination in astrology, tarot, and the like. It does not explain the effects of

magic in invoking forces, changing patterns through ritual, effecting healing or fulfilling desires.

While the description of synchronicity as an "acausal principal" is good, the activity of the "psychoid archetypes" come perilously close to a restatement of the idea of the spirit world or the astral plane, and Jung knew it. We suspect (as have others) that he used the terms collective unconscious and synchronicity to describe "occult" experiences that he had had himself and dealt with clinically while avoiding what would have been the damaging stigma of being labeled a psychical researcher.

Jung also stated that the beings that he spoke to during his "active imagination" sessions were intelligent entities with an independent existence outside his own mind.

In the year 1916, entities began invading his house. His children, the staff and Jung himself observed phantom figures in the house as well as poltergeist phenomena. This and other phenomena inspired him to write the *Seven Sermons to the Dead,* a work that he implies was produced almost in a mediumistic state.

From looking at this work and many of his letters that were published after his death, it is clear that he was far more ambivalent on the subject of spirits than his public statements suggested. He did "psychologize" occult phenomena at the beginning of his career, but did so less and less as he became older. Perhaps the most direct reference to his personal beliefs can be found in one of the above-mentioned letters:

> I once discussed the proof of identity for a long time with a friend of William James, Professor Hyslop, in New York. He admitted that, all things considered, all these metapsychic phenomena could be explained better by the hypothesis of spirits than by the qualities and peculiarities of the unconscious. And here, on the basis of my own experience, I am bound to concede he is right. In each individual case I must of necessity be

skeptical, but in the long run I have to admit that the spirit hypothesis yields better results in practice than any other.

THE DEMONS & THE BEAST

The other authority most quoted to support the "in your head" point of view is The Beast himself, Aleister Crowley. In the year 1903, he published a new edition in English of the *Goetia*, a book that is first cousin to the Grimoires collected here, but much older. As an introduction to this book, he wrote a little essay entitled *The Initiated Interpretation of Ceremonial Magick*. In it, he tried to relate the phenomena attendant to ceremonial practice to a combination of psychology and Oriental solipsism. The most often quoted remark from this essay is the one that I blame for this misunderstanding of Crowley's actual stated position. It is this:

> But can any of the effects described in this our book Goetia be obtained, and if so, can you give a rational explanation of the circumstances? Say you so?
> I can and will.
> The spirits of the Goetia are portions of the human brain.

Voila. From the pen of the premier practitioner of this century, what appears to be the flat statement that the demons are in your head. But wait. Crowley did indeed write this, but it is usually taken slightly out of context. On the very first page of this essay he says:

> I am not concerned to deny the objective reality of all "magical" phenomena; if they are illusions, they are at least as real as many unquestioned facts of daily life; and, if we follow Herbert Spencer, they are at least evidence of some cause.

The problems here are multiple. First, Crowley, as usual, is smarter than his audience. He was at the time, deep in the study of Eastern thought with his friend Allan Bennett and was speaking in a sophisticated way of the Buddhist concept of world/mind indivisibility. "All is mind." This has tended to be interpreted by readers in terms of pop psychology, which of course did not exist in Crowley's time. Then too, this was still the heyday of spiritualism, which Crowley viewed with a combination of contempt and (in our opinion) jealousy. He did not want to be seen as another fool writing about spirits. The long and short of it was that he was just a little too clever in his presentation to be entirely clear in his meaning, not the last time this was to happen to him.

To set the matter as straight as it will get, here he is in his very last book, *Magick Without Tears* (New Falcon Publications), written only a few years before his death, referring to the "objective existence" of the Holy Guardian Angel:

> ...the Angel is an actual individual with his own Universe, exactly as a man is; or, for the matter of that, a bluebottle. He is not a mere abstraction, a selection from and exaltation of one's own favourite qualities, as the "Higher Self" seems to be...
>
> Now do remember this: it is the guarantee of wholesomeness in any Invocation that there should be *contact with another*. It is better to conjure up the most obnoxious demons from the most noisome pit of Hell than to take one's own excitations for divine benediction; if only because there was never a demon yet so atrocious as that same old ego.

He goes on to warn that the practice of "conjuring yourself" (which he compares to masturbation) can lead to delusory ego inflation—a result we have observed more times than we've liked.

CHAPTER NINE

Modern Practices — Personal Testimony

[The material in this section includes more of S. Jason Black's personal experiences.]

Crowley and Jung aside, I would like to relate some of my own experiences regarding the practices described in this book.

I will begin with some of experiences I have had with the art of evocation, and finish with a pact-working that I performed, though different from the specific rituals in this book.

About ten years ago I was in the midst of one of my early experiments in ceremonial magic. I had acquired or made the required ritual equipment and had created a nine-foot circle that could be folded up and stored away instead of having to be recreated each time it was needed. As a result, it was no great trouble to perform rituals on a nightly basis, since only minimal preparation was needed. I had decided on a planetary working as most appropriate to my needs, and chose the intelligence of Venus (Hagiel) as the spirit to call up.

I would perform a basic evocation ritual about an hour before going to bed each night, beginning and ending with the Golden Dawn banishing ritual and including the planetary incense and proper color scheme. After the invocation, I would sit in the circle and attempt to visualize the spirit. At first, little happened, but with each successive ritual the trance that I entered became a little deeper, until I was regularly experiencing what I can only describe as a joyful glow rather like being on a good mood-lifter.

For about two weeks I continued this procedure. Each time I made my requests to the spirit I had yet to see. Then, one night, I laid out the circle, lit the candles and prepared for the usual routine when I stopped cold right in the middle of the pentagram ritual. I had the sensation—and I'm afraid that I'm helpless to describe it any better—that something enormous had just come into the room. Please let me emphasize that this was *not* a "mood." It was a physical sensation that, had I not rooted myself in the circle, would have backed me against the wall.

I literally felt as though an elephant had walked into the room. As I was standing, the entire front of my body began to buzz from head to foot as though I was being pressed against a six-foot vibrator; and something seemed to be *forming* in the space outside the circle directly in front of me.

This started as a kind of narrowing of the buzzing sensation (again, I apologize for the obscurity of my description) to a point on the floor in front of me. I was overcome with a sense of expectancy that amounted almost to panic. This feeling increased to the point that I was about to run out of the room when suddenly a pile of record albums that were laid flat on the floor, and probably weighed about twenty pounds, flipped over with a loud *whump*. These albums were not balanced on their spines, but were levered by an unseen agency, from a point resting on their backs, to resting on their fronts, something that I would have had to get down on my knees and use both hands to accomplish myself.

Immediately after this little kinetic demonstration, a blob of light formed on the floor in front of the circle. It stayed there for about thirty seconds, then formed into a ball and rose slowly into the air in front of me to a point about four feet off the ground. It hung there for an additional twenty seconds or so and then vanished.

(I lived at the time in a small apartment at the back of a building facing away from the street. Automobile headlights never reached the interior of my home and if they had they would not have made cohesive balls of light that hung suspended in the air. In addition, my apartment was equipped with blackout shades, which were completely opaque and could block out all light even at noon on a summer day.)

When the light vanished, so did the fear. The presence was still in the room, however, and I was at a loss as to what to do. In the end, I broke what most people consider a cardinal rule and requested the spirit to communicate with me in whatever way it could. I then stepped out of the circle without banishing and went to bed. When I turned off the light and lay down, I saw (as clearly as possible under the circumstances) a shifting shape of blackness floating above me. I was still excited, but not afraid. Considering my agitation, I didn't see how I could possibly sleep.

I went instantly to sleep.

I awoke around 3:00 AM, having the distinct and intense recollection of talking to someone for a very long time about something very important to my life and well being. Do I even need to say that I couldn't remember a word of it? The room was empty of disembodied presences and I eventually drifted back to sleep.

The day after this event the Venus effect kicked in. Strangers would, it seemed, come for miles to make my acquaintance. I would be pestered in bars, restaurants and shopping malls by people who thought (wrongly) that I was the friendliest, most wholesome person in the state and they ought to become my friend. One man even came to my door looking for someone who used to live in my apartment. He decided to tell his troubles to me for several hours instead and wanted to pursue a further acquaintance. I politely declined.

The upside to this was that my sex life improved spectacularly, but with every emotionally needy person within a hundred miles "just happening" to meet me when they needed someone like me. It wasn't worth it. I counted the operation a success, and convinced that ceremonial magic lived up to its advertising, destroyed the Venus talisman.

The second example is a bit less spectacular when it comes to phenomena, but much more successful in the practical sense. It also is far more typical of the experience with magic than the first story.

INFERNAL ALLY

I had been doing an extended working with the Goetic demon Marchosias, who appears, according to the *Lesser Key of Solomon*, as a great wolf with the wings of a gryphon and is said to be a "strong fighter" on behalf of the magician.

By this time I had altered my method of working slightly. If I had decided that the "force" or "spirit" was well disposed toward me (and I had come to such a conclusion about Marchosias), I would dispense with a circle and concentrate on the goal of communication rather than protection. I did this by putting myself into an auto-hypnotic trance before an altar containing the sigil of the spirit and whatever other material I thought necessary. This technique resembled the Theurgy of the Renaissance magicians more than the methodology of the Grimoires. It also closely resembles Tantrik devotional Yoga.

I had been calling up this particular spirit for some little while with what I considered satisfactory results: that is, things that I wanted to happen, happened and information that I needed, I obtained—either clairvoyantly or through "coincidence."

I was "secure" in the job I had, but I felt underpaid and dissatisfied. Not an unusual situation I'm sure. I had been in the habit of rising early and performing the evocation after I bathed and before going to work. On the morning in question, I was feeling particularly frustrated about my financial situation, as well as my emotional and physical condition. I needed money, I was bored and out of shape. Almost more than the money, I wanted a membership in one of the well-appointed health clubs that are common in the Los Angeles area and which, at the time, I could not afford. This was the subject of my particular bitch to the spirit that morning.

I went through the usual routine. I recall that the meditation, or trance portion, was particularly poor that morning. I complained to the spirit (and I think this is important) *verbally*, just as though I were talking to a person in the room with me who knew nothing about my situation. I spoke in considerable detail. I said, in brief, that I needed a new job that paid me a decent wage, and especially, I wanted a gym membership so that I could get myself back into physical shape again. Ordinary requests to be sure, but ones beyond my power to fulfill at the time. Having complained at length, I found it was time to go to work, performed a hasty closing and left.

When I arrived at the office (I was working at a Hollywood talent agency at the time), I opened up as usual and took the numerous phone messages from the answering service. When the office officially opened for business about forty minutes later, I was deeply absorbed in fielding the hundreds of calls from actors and casting directors when I got a call from one of our actress clients who wanted to talk to me. She began by asking me if I was satisfied where I was working. I said that I liked the people but the money was lousy and I was going nowhere. Well, she said, there was a close friend of hers who was about to open the new national office of a broadcasting professional organization and he was looking for someone with exactly my background and skills. She gave me a number to call, which I did as soon as I had the time.

I interviewed during lunch the next day and was hired immediately. The salary was more than four times what I was previously making and the new office was almost ten miles closer to my home. As I was leaving, he said, "By the way, there's a new health club opening a block away from the office and I'm paying half the membership for any employees interested."

The phone call that got me the interview came within two hours of the evocation ritual. The complete fulfillment of all my requests came within thirty hours.

In this case there were no floating lights, no spirits talking to me in dreams, only the straightforward operation and the straightforward result. This is the way such things usually go. Phenomena sporadically occur, but the appearance of floating lights or poltergeist phenomena—although impressive to the practitioner (to put it mildly)—do not presage success in your goals. Conversely, even though there were no subjective or objective changes in my environment during the above operation, I *operated under the assumption* that there was an alien intelligence present that was well disposed to me and capable of helping me, and behaved accordingly. The results were entirely consonant with that assumption, whether valid or not.

DEMONIC OBSESSION

The last little ghost story I have to tell is a cautionary one. Obviously, I am not one of those people who constantly warns the interested person how dangerous occult practice is. I firmly believe that the techniques of magic, going back into the mists of prehistory, are man's birthright and his to use if he has the talent. However, the powers that one calls up, if successful in one's operation, are quite real—whatever you choose to believe they are—and are capable of wreaking havoc in an extremely persuasive and unpleasant way if hostile.

In this case, the operation began as an experiment. It was done in a "lets try this" spirit, without any specific need that I can recall. Occult phenomena was what I wanted and occult phenomena was what I got.

At this time, I was living in Hollywood, sharing an apartment with a girl I'll call Susan. She was also involved in magic, but in a rather fluffy sort of way, being more concerned about justifying her psychotic behavior than with spiritual development. I came up with the idea of evoking the solar demon Sorath, identified by Rudolf Steiner among others as the Beast in the Apocalypse of St. John.

I laid down a circle, as in the first example, with the difference that Susan was in the circle with me and it was done in broad daylight rather than at night. I followed the procedure as before, and asked Susan to act as a "skryer" along with me so that we could compare clairvoyant visions when the ritual was over.

After I had read the invocation several times, I commanded the spirit to appear in the triangle before me. At first nothing happened. Then, I began to feel that tingling along my face and body that I came to associate with psychic manifestation. It was then that the first interesting thing happened—the room went cold.

It was the middle of a Sunday afternoon in late August. We were in, and had been in for some weeks, one of those heat waves that hit Southern California typically at the end of summer. There was no air-conditioning in our apartment, and the temperature outside was over one hundred.

In spite of the physical conditions, in a matter of seconds the room became so cold that the sweat dried on our skins and we became very uncomfortable. We could both feel a cold breeze blowing over us from the direction of the triangle. By this time spirit phenomena no longer frightened me, so I was very pleased by this event.

I addressed the presumed spirit politely, welcoming it and requesting it's cooperation. I requested that it link itself with the talisman that I had prepared, and lend us the benefit of it's influence. Since it was supposed to be solar in nature, I supposed this influence to be beneficial.

We then proceeded to the skrying session and afterwards closed the ceremony after calling upon the spirit to depart.

The visions, when we compared them, weren't terribly impressive. I saw a pattern of black and gold and she saw a lion. The one was obscure and the other stereotyped.

That night, I dreamed of the same swirling pattern of black and gold, with a deep voice saying something portentous (which I couldn't remember). Then I walked down a long street to meet a beautiful man with golden hair, dressed entirely in black. He led me to a cliff that overlooked the ocean where I saw a fleet of flying saucers (solar disks) lifting off the beach into the sky. A good dream, full of nifty symbols appropriate to the ritual, but hardly supernatural.

The next day my roommate was talking to a friend of hers in New York. When she hung up the phone she had an odd look on her face and I asked her what was wrong. She said that her girlfriend had found her pet snake dead in its terrarium the day before, at about the time we were performing the evocation.

The snake was named Sorath.

This seems rather more sinister in retrospect than it did at the time. I simply assumed that it was a piece of synchronicity that meant the magical operation was working.

I evoked the demon Sorath twice more, with little in the way of phenomena except increasingly disturbing dreams at night. Then, about a week after the initial ritual, I had the experience that has given me such sympathy with St. Anthony.

THE DEMON COMES CALLING

I had just come home from work and Susan was vegged out on pot and beer, watching Wheel of Fortune on television. It was late and I relaxed in a recliner and tried to ignore what was on TV. I was in the chair only a moment when I began to have one of the strongest trance experiences of my life.

I felt as though I had been injected with some kind of powerful tranquilizer that gave my body an utterly relaxed, glowing feeling, at the same time sharpening my senses so that colors were brighter, objects more "real" than they were a moment before. Since this was hardly a common occurrence, I knew that I was at last getting positive results from the Sorath operation.

"Susan," I said, "I'm going into a trance. Something's happening."

"That's nice," she said, completely stoned.

I headed toward my bedroom and stopped off at the bathroom first. Still dizzy from the trance state that continued to increase as I walked, I stood at the toilet and began to relieve myself.

Blue light began crawling across the walls.

I informed my roommate of this, only to get the same cabbage-like response.

I retired to my bedroom to deal privately with whatever was happening to me. I turned on the ceiling light and saw the flowing blue light follow me into the room and solidify into an unchanging shape hanging just below the ceiling. The ceiling light in that room was very bright, so much so that I rarely used it, yet it did nothing to dim or affect the brightness or sharpness of the blue-light-thing. I closed my eyes, I shook my head, I spun around, I turned the lights off and on. I did everything that I could think of to see if I was experiencing "spots before my eyes."

The blue light figure (which looked something like a Chinese ideogram in a circle) remained absolutely stationary and unchanging, visible whether the light was on or off. Far from being frightened by what was happening, I thought it a wonderful chance to communicate with what I had called up.

I kept the light on, lay down on my bed and waited.

And waited. And waited.

Nothing happened, nothing changed.

Finally, I actually began to read a book. I suppose that it's possible to become bored with anything.

Ultimately, *an hour and a half* after the phenomena began, I addressed the enigmatic light and said that if it wanted to communicate, it was welcome to do so. I was at a loss as to what it wanted or how to talk to it. I turned out the light and went to bed.

I found myself in an enormous subterranean vault. There were fifty-foot Gothic arches of carved gray stone, the relief worn almost smooth by time. The arches led into darkness. The central area, where I was standing, was lit by a dim, evenly distributed sourceless light. In the center of the vault was an ancient-looking chest or cask carved from stone.

The sight of this cask filled me with greater terror than I have ever felt in my life. I *knew* that it was about to open and that I had to stop it or a disaster would befall. I moved toward it and screamed "stop!" just as the lid was flung to the floor as though it was made of plastic instead of heavy stone.

Instantly there appeared before the casket a figure out of an oriental nightmare. Dressed in a elegant red satin robe embroidered with dragons done in gold thread was one of the most threatening and ugly things I have ever seen, dreaming or waking. It was wiry, no taller than I was, with greenish gray skin and a body made for pure destruction. It's hands had sharp, seven-inch claws on each finger and it had a mouth that split its skull literally from ear to ear, filled with teeth like a shark. It was completely hairless and had compelling golden eyes (the only beautiful thing about it) filled with mad intelligence.

And it was *radiant.*

Even though we were in a dark space and it didn't glow in any way having to do with light, I was unable to look at it for more than a second at a time. My eyes would water and my eyelids squint shut automatically exactly as though I were looking into a klieg light or the sun.

When this thing appeared, it looked at me and laughed. Its voice was the most inhuman thing about it. If a giant pipe organ had learned to talk, that is what it would sound like. It said some things to me in a voice that I felt more than heard, laughed again and I "woke up."

It was daylight. I was bathed in sweat and as soon as I became fully aware I became hysterical. I felt emotionally and physically shattered to a degree that I can hardly begin to describe. I continued crying for the rest of the day. I was absolutely unable to recover my composure. Bodily, I felt as though I had been "worked over." My limbs hurt, I felt weak and had a severe headache.

I wasn't able to function until the following day, when at least I was able to stop crying. Then I destroyed the talisman and everything to do with the Sorath operation. I cleansed myself ritually as best I could, but remained depressed and on the verge of panic and hysteria for another two weeks.

I did not call up Sorath again.

What happened here? As with so much "occult" or "psychic" phenomena, ultimately I simply don't know. This is one of a very few "attacks" that I have experienced in the course of my occult experimentation. I include it here because I want the new practitioner to understand that, whether he believes in "spirits" or not, the legends of predatory demons and fatal spells come from an *experi-*

enced reality and something like the above could occur, as it did with me, just when you feel most secure.

The intelligences that the magician calls up are often the wild forces of nature and sometimes have no more morality or gentleness than a tiger. You are dealing with the primitive world, the forces and beings that created and operate "nature." That being the case, the serious practitioner sometimes encounters more than he bargains for.

The above experiences are examples of the wilder, more sensational side of magic. It should be obvious though, that spectacular phenomena and useful practical results don't always go together.

Two comments before I go on:

First, those who are familiar with the traditions of magic and witchcraft may say that I invited problems by dealing with the "demon" outside of a circle. My reply to this is that:

1. The magic circle seems to be a post-classical development. The majority of magical techniques outside Europe do not use such a device.

2. I assure you that in practice, if a real manifestation occurs and is hostile, you will wind up having to deal with it outside the protection of a circle. If you cannot weather such an experience and learn from it, don't take up the practice of magic.

I'd like to quote once again the redoubtable Aleister Crowley regarding what I learn from such events:

"But it does encourage one—it is useless to deny it—to be knocked down by a demon of whose existence one was not really quite sure."

A Bargain Made

Since this is a book about pacts as well as about the conjuration of demons, I also have a personal story regarding the only pact operation that I have done to date. This took place around eight years ago, during a period in my life when I was under constant and intense emotional stress. I won't bore you with the background, but I was suffering from clinical depression and having anxiety attacks on a regular basis. These attacks took a particularly violent and physical form. I would be walking or driving someplace, and suddenly feel a tightness around my solar plexus like a vibrating steel band. I would all but cease to be able to breathe, my vision would start to blur and the muscles around my mouth would lock in a *rictus* so that I was unable to talk. Both of my hands would go numb and usually my feet as well. This experience could last anywhere from ten minutes to half an hour. The first time that I had the experience I was in a shopping mall and I thought I was having a heart attack. When a friend witnessed one of these attacks, he thought I was having a stroke.

Imagine the fun of having such an attack while driving on the freeway.

At any rate, this should give the reader a good idea of my psycho-physical state at the time. I needed a very *large* change in my life and couldn't see how to make it happen.

This was during the period when I was first experimenting with Goetic conjuration, and my experiences had been interesting but uneven. I was desperate enough in my circumstances to try something radical, and like Goethe's Faust, felt I had little to lose.

I selected two of the Princes of Hell that I thought would be of benefit in my situation and drafted two pacts, one for each. These were not of the soul-selling variety and were highly legalistic, consisting of very small writing covering nearly both sides of rather large sheets of parchment, accompanied by the appropriate pantacles and sigils.

I found this activity strangely disturbing. It should have been made clear to the reader by now that I am no believer in Little Lord Jesus. Even so, I was preparing for an operation that struck right at the heart of the psychological and spiritual taboos ground into us by our Judeo-Christian culture and the fear that was developing in me had nothing to do with my rational conscious attitudes.

I prepared for the ritual as usual, laying down the circle and triangle, purifying the work space with water and incense, making sure all the tools that I needed—which in this case included a small knife to draw blood—were ready at hand.

When the night came—which appropriately enough was April 30th, Walpurgis Nacht—I entered the circle and began the conjuration. With each passing moment, I became more nervous. I trembled. I sweated. I was reacting like a midwestern Sunday school teacher. All of the superstitious fears instilled by my Protestant upbringing and the culture that I was born into rose to the surface.

Despite my nervousness, the ritual was rather uneventful. There were no bizarre manifestations and the only communication that I had with the "spirits" was through a pendulum (a device that I have found *very* useful). The demon Princes, if they were there at all, signaled (through the pendulum) that the conditions of the pacts were acceptable, and that I should consider them signed. I then stuck my finger with the knife, took up a quill pen and signed my own name on the documents in blood.

Well, nothing much happened.

My life continued on its tedious course and so did my anxiety attacks. There were no dreams or omens. I was disappointed.

About a week later, I was having lunch with a friend and was discussing my situation and the conjuration that I had attempted and that I concluded it was a flat failure. I told him basically that I probably should not have done it in the first place.

Rather to my surprise, he disagreed. He pointed out to me that demons are traditionally the embodiment of natural forces and that in many ancient religious traditions demons, or their equivalent, taught man the arts of civilization. In effect, cities, science and the arts are the work of demons and what I tried to do was not only appropriate and traditionally valid, but the natural thing to do.

The two little blue-haired ladies at the table next to us seemed to find this conversation distracting.

I agreed with this point of view enthusiastically. I said that I probably had botched the conjuration because of my hesitancy and would re-attempt it at my first opportunity.

That, as events were to prove, was the moment that I *really* signed the pacts.

I was in my car, driving up the freeway back home when the pain started. The bones in my legs and arms began to throb in unison and I developed a splitting headache. My strength began to ebb away and driving became very nearly torture.

When I arrived home half an hour later, I parked the car with some difficulty, and dragged myself into my apartment building. I lived in a third floor walk-up and for a bad moment didn't think that I was going to make it to my apartment. I unlocked the door, went in and was literally struck down.

My knees buckled and I thought that I was going to lose consciousness. I crawled to my bedroom, got in bed and remained there for five days.

What I experienced was unlike any illness I have ever had before or since. There was no fever or nausea, like one would associate with the flu, just an intense pain in my limbs and an attendant weakness that was so great that I literally could not get up. I had to crawl to the bathroom to relieve myself or get water, and for all intents and purposes, didn't eat during this entire time. There were times when I thought that I might die, and just when I was about to call someone to take me to the hospital, the symptoms would lessen a bit. I was unable to think clearly, as though there was static in my brain.

Then it stopped.

One day I was helpless, the next, I woke up free of all symptoms and seven pounds lighter.

This had happened in the springtime, hardly flu season, so I began asking around to see if anyone else had gotten this peculiar illness. I described the experience to literally dozens of people and not only had no one had what I described, but they didn't know anyone that had. Several of these people were experienced nurses and even they had no idea what it might have been. I wrote the experience off as something that I'd never figure out.

A Bargain Kept

Suddenly, my life began to transform.

Within days of my "illness" my work situation improved drastically. So did my income. My living situation changed for the better and, while I was still thanking fate for my recently increased income, I was offered still another job—and in a city that I had been wanting to move to, but hadn't been able to do so.

Most importantly, I found, or rather, was given, the man that cured my depression and panic attacks.

I had applied to a local counseling center to find some help with these problems and had been put on a waiting list. Some months went by and I had all but forgotten that I had done it. Then the phone call came telling me I had been assigned a therapist. To get to the point, this man, as it turned out, came from almost exactly my background and had had the same symptoms himself at one time. Only those of you who have been forced to get a therapist by the roll of the dice in a "charitable" situation know what a miracle it was getting the right man under those circumstances.

The upshot was that my depression was dealt with and the panic syndrome disappeared, never to return.

You will have to agree that even though there were no obviously supernatural happenings involved, the cluster of events, taken in order and as a whole, are rather weird.

STRANGE COINCIDENCE

As I pointed out earlier, magic usually works through "synchronicity," or unusual coincidence, rather than the casual breaking of physical laws. You perform the proper actions—"spells" if you will—and what you want to happen "just happens." What I wanted and needed to happen, "just happened" after the pact-working, things that I could not make happen before. Of course, the person determined to tear this story apart can do it with very little trouble, by (magically) invoking "coincidence" and "selective attention."

There is no real way I can counter that argument, except to say that if I were into self-deception, I would still be attending the Presbyterian Church, and when I put my car key into the ignition the hundredth time and it starts the hundredth time, coincidence is not relevant.

What about the illness? Again, it could be argued that I "just happened" to get sick at a time that *seemed* to be meaningful and if I had continued inquiring, I would have found out what the illness "really" was. Well, maybe. But I personally suspect that, considering the emotional state I was in at the time, there is another possible model.

I think that the pact ritual, which breaks so very many cultural taboos, released something deep inside me and the psychic poisons—for want of a better term—were released from their dammed-up state and flooded my system all at once. I have had similar experiences since, but none so devastating. When the "sickness" left me, I was suddenly empowered and everything that I needed (and had requested) "miraculously" occurred.

This, in my opinion, is a good demonstration of the primordial power of the idea of a pact with a supernatural force. Whether or not there were demonic intelligences involved, the act itself was so powerful and disturbing to my system that the whole course of my life took an abrupt turn. It is this personal empowerment that is threatening to a monotheistic/authoritarian establishment, hence the taboos and fairy tales of magicians damned to hell.

As a footnote, the pacts made in the above ritual were not lifelong. They were ritually dissolved a few years later when my life entered another phase and they no longer seemed relevant.

Since we have covered (roughly) the historical background of the three Grimoires and related some personal experiences with this style of magic, it is time to make some remarks on the personages this material revolves around: the Devil and his demons.

CHAPTER TEN

The Fall From Heaven

ORIGINS OF THE DEVIL

A number of comprehensive histories of the Devil have been written from various points of view, some running to several volumes. What is clear from all of them is that Lucifer is not entirely a biblical character. Like Jesus, he is based on primeval myth with a thin Jewish/Roman/Christian overlay.

There are several deities that were worshipped throughout the Roman empire that are good candidates for the original pre-Christian devil. Thanks—once again—to remarks by Aleister Crowley, many people, especially "neo-pagans," assert that the Devil is simply Pan. They say that the early Christians took this friendly forest god, with his pipes and perpetual hard-on, and turned him into the Devil. They go further and state that there is no Devil, that He is purely a Christian invention.

This looks reasonable on the face of it—if you don't know anything about history.

First of all, Pan was not the happy little god that one sees on greeting cards and in children's books. This is the castrated version that has been perpetuated by our culture, and the "neo-pagans" seem to have bought into it. He was in fact, along with Silenus and a number of other entities, a nature god, a god of dark forests and wild beasts. The fact that a direct confrontation with Pan was supposed to drive people mad says something about his nature.

Even with this violent aspect restored, however, Pan and his cult do not match up at all well with the myth and worship of the Fallen One.

Others do.

To properly understand this, we need to examine the traditional character and powers of Lucifer, leaving aside both Milton and the rantings of the fundamentalists.

Lucifer (or *Iblis* to the Moslems) is a supernatural entity of immense age and power who, for reasons rather obscure, fell into conflict with the Supreme Being. We are using the monotheistic myth here of course. Because of this conflict, he and his supporters were tossed out of "Heaven" and made a new camp for themselves elsewhere.

This Supreme Being (Jehovah or Allah, pick one) was a strict disciplinarian when it came to His creation. He especially wanted mankind kept fettered and in ignorance. This, of course, was for mankind's own good. It became the goal of Lucifer/Iblis to disrupt this rigid order and set up his own, looser organization. He began this project by offering man the things that "God" forbade him. This led to the "fall of man" and the teaching to mankind of various "occult" arts which led to the rise of civilization. Whether you see this as a bad thing or not depends largely on whether you have ever had to live naked in the woods with no toilet paper.

So, in return for allegiance and various other forms of payment (like any other ancient god), the Devil will grant magical powers, knowledge, beauty, etc. etc. That is one half of the picture.

On the other side we have Satan the Adversary (for the Jews, Satan meant "accuser" and was an *office*, not a being), who spreads disease, heresy, destroys civilizations (a lot like Jehovah) and does a multitude of other unpleasant things. This double "light-bringing" and destructive aspect, removed from the superstitious trappings of modern religion, is a common characteristic of all deities that come from a polytheistic source, including the Old Testament version of Jehovah.

SEX & THE DEVIL

In our culture the Devil also presides over sexuality and artistic creativity. Both sex and beauty are considered potentially, if not intrinsically, evil, unless rigidly controlled by the Church or State. This attitude represses natural urges and abilities in people, creating emotional devastation which in turn often inspires a greater need for the Church or State.

This cycle of temptation/fulfillment/guilt has created a psychological maelstrom among some segments of the population in the United States. This is expressed in the rage and envy vented from the pulpit against rock stars, artists, writers, even scientists. The target is anyone who they suspect has freed themselves from the Christian emotional bind (or as Reich called it, emotional plague), or worse yet, has never been in it. These people are labeled as "satanic" and some (like rock stars) are even accused of literal Devil-worship.

CONSPIRACY FROM THE ABYSS

Another expression of this illness is the current urban myth of a world-wide satanic conspiracy. This nonsense has been exploded dozens of times in major newspapers and magazines over the years, but if you don't read—or even if you do—you don't have to pay attention to facts. Thousands of the half-educated middle class firmly believe that there is an *organized* underground that routinely performs human sacrifice many times a year with absolutely no trace of the bodies. (It has been pointed out that the white middle-class is more susceptible to this kind of fear because they are more vulnerable. The poor have nowhere to fall and the rich are too powerful to be bothered.) They have supposedly been up to this throughout this century without *ever* being caught. (According to an FBI investigation on Satanic crime no such conspiracy exists, a fact which this movement ignores.)

This is "explained" by asserting that there is a network of satanic lawyers, doctors, travel agents, preschools, etc., all identifiable by secret symbols in the Yellow Pages. Thus, babies are born and raised without birth certificates, payoffs are made, and everyone is protected. What is significant about this delusion (which has recurred throughout human history and is called the "blood libel") is that it mirrors exactly what fundamentalist Christians themselves do. They *actually have* fundamentalist lawyers, doctors, TV repairmen, travel agents, etc. who can be identified by "secret symbols" in the Yellow Pages. If you don't believe us, just let your fingers do the walking and look for that little fish.

What all of this says is that basically, in a culture with an authoritarian mythology, the Devil is the god of the repressed. Thus painters and photographers who do all those "dirty" nudes and sexy, sweaty rock stars dressed in leather and covered with tribal tattoos are all genuinely sons of the Devil.

But once again, *who really is* this Devil?

DIONYSUS, SON OF GOD

Even before Jesus was a twinkle in Joseph's eye, there was a secret and widespread cult that was celebrated throughout the Mediterranean world. They had secret initiations, and met at night in wild places hidden from prying eyes. They cut the throats of black goats in offering to their god, took intoxicants and indulged in ritual sodomy to commemorate a similar act supposedly performed by the deity. The celebrants would experience spirit possession and run naked through the wilderness bringing down deer and wild sheep with their bare hands and eating them raw. Sound familiar? If not, I refer you to the published accounts of the European witch trials available at any bookstore or library.

The god referred to is, of course, Dionysus.

Dionysus, more than any other classical deity, fits the figure, function and worship of Lucifer. He is beautiful, bisexual and a master of undisciplined "black" magic. His presence divests people of their repressions and cultural programming, a truly horrible thing in the eyes of Christians and pre-Christian Romans. He is capable of great love and sensuality toward his followers and insensate cruelty toward his enemies (or perhaps, the enemies of nature).

He also has horns.

The ultimate origins of the cult of Dionysus are at present unclear. The Romans considered him Greek. The Greeks however, also considered him foreign and some myths state categorically that he came from "the East."

He may have literally done so.

The French author Alain Danielou in his book, *Shiva and Dionysus* contends that the cults of the Indian Shiva and the Greek Dionysus may have had the same origins. He points out the remarkable similarity between the two deities; their androgynous appearance, the primitive emotional violence of their rites, the two-sided loving/destructive function.

Shiva is also the god of intoxication. Wherever he goes he always has his drug jar at his side. In addition, the two gods share an eerie similarity in the various titles that they were given: *Eriboas* (Greek) and *Rudra* (Hindu) both mean "Howler." Dionysus was supposed to come from, or live on, Mt. Nysa, and there were several mountains in India with that name. One of the Indian titles of Shiva is *Nisah*.

Shiva was, in Hindu myth, also the creator and first teacher of Tantra. The majority of the Hindu Tantras are even written as dialogues between Shiva and his consort.

The similarity between Tantrik practice and European black magic has already been pointed out, as well as the virtual identity of the Dionysian revels and the Sabbat.

THE THIRD EYE OF LUCIFER

As an interesting sidelight to the Shiva/Dionysus/Lucifer connection we make note of one of the accounts of the Holy Grail, beloved of medieval mystics. In *Parzival*, the Grail Stone (it was originally described as a stone, not a cup) was an emerald that fell from the brow of Lucifer as he was hurled to Earth by Jehovah. This would correspond to the idea of the "third eye" or Ajna chakra. What is the gift that one who finds the Grail expects to receive? It is never clearly stated. But considering the symbolism of the story, it is reasonable to assume that the successful seeker is given the *spiritual perception of an archangel.* Was this not the goal of Faust? There is said to be a pearl in the forehead of Shiva called the *Urna,* which enabled him to perceive eternity. Is this an interesting parallel? Or did some crusader or trader bring this tradition back from the East and create the beginnings of Grail mysticism?

There is another, perhaps even more central precursor to the Christian Devil: Prometheus the Firebringer.

THE ORIGINAL LIGHT-BRINGER

Here we have a parallel with the Christian story that is very close indeed. Prometheus the Titan, seeing what a sad plight mankind was in—living in darkness—resolved to defy the other gods and bring man the gift of fire. He climbs to the home of the gods and steals fire in a tube, carefully carrying it down to Earth again. He presents the fire to Man and teaches the people of the world how to use this gift. The inhabitants of Earth now had warmth and the ability to cook food and were appropriately grateful. The gods, however, were not pleased.

They outlawed Prometheus, and as punishment chained him to a rock in the wilderness. To torment him, they placed with him two enormous carrion birds that would rip at his body eternally, while he eternally healed—so that they could begin again.

Here we have a powerful supernatural being bringing a forbidden and life-changing boon to the human race. Like Lucifer, he is literally the "light-bringer." Also like Lucifer he is cast out of Heaven and relegated to a kind of Hell. Of course, all of this is done in a rather different order than in the Christian myth, but the essential elements are the same. The big difference is that Prometheus was looked upon as a hero and Lucifer, for performing the same kind of service ("...you shall be as gods...") is looked upon as the incarnation of evil. This says something deeply disturbing about our attitude toward the universe and our place in it.

We should point out a major irony. Not only did Dionysus and Prometheus contribute to the myth of the Devil, but they were equally major contributors to the Jesus myth as well. Both gods came to Earth and brought new knowledge to Man. Both "died" for the effort and one (Dionysus) was resurrected and ascended to heaven. These are only two of nearly a dozen "dying gods" whose cults were looted (and then wiped out) to create Christianity.

Prometheus was the subject of a major revival on two occasions. First, Milton's Satan has been widely compared to Prometheus in his heroic attitude of unrepentant rebellion and assertion of self over authority. Milton himself would be appalled by this, but as Blake said, he was obviously "...of the Devil's party without knowing it."

The second revival came during the Romantic period when Byron and Shelly, as well as numerous lesser lights, devoted major works to the Firebringer. While these works weren't openly Satanic in form, they were in spirit, and when someone of the period was described as "Byronic" what was meant was "devilish." Those of you who have read *Frankenstein* might also recall that it was subtitled "The Modern Prometheus."

This has been but a thumbnail history of the Fallen Angel. Besides the influences listed, there were Gnostic, Persian and possibly Egyptian contributions as well. The point is that the mythological and theological traditions of the Devil are not just Christian fabrications. They go back into the mists of history and should be carefully studied, not rejected, by the serious student of the occult.

DEMONOLOGY

Having covered, in a brief way, the birth of Satan, it is time to examine a subject less mythological and much more phenomenological: the Principalities and Powers, the Lords of Darkness, the demons themselves.

Except for the veneer that individual religions place over it, the concept of demons is nearly the same now as it was in ancient Mesopotamia. The fundamental definition of a demon, without theological baggage, is a non-human entity of great intelligence and power, existing as mind and spirit, and capable of influencing the material world. To someone raised Muslim or Christian, this definition will seem much too broad. However, for the magician, both now and in the past, the operational attitude toward demons has more to do with the classical past than the Christian present.

In ancient times and during the first centuries AD when the *Corpus Hermeticum* was written, all demons—good and bad—were considered as a single class. If a demon was hostile or "evil" it was referred to as a *cacodemon*. The "angels" of the Biblical mythology hadn't been integrated into the mainstream yet, and simply came to replace the demons as the principal supernatural beings that interacted with man.

The political motivation for this, as with so much of the Christian structure, is obvious. Christianity created the myth of the soul-stealing demon to quash magical practice outside the Church. Even in the Grimoires written in the Judeo-Christian tradition, one can see a scrap of the old attitude remaining. For example, in the *Goetia*, several of the Princes of Hell are described as "good by nature" or "well disposed to the Exorcist."

In the traditional world-view, the universe is filled with intelligence. This intelligence manifests itself on all levels of nature: from animals—of which man is the highest—to spirits or pure mind—of which "gods" are the highest—and of which the elementals and the "demons of the air" are the closest to man.

Prejudice and terminology make it is difficult to write about demonology without sounding incoherent or foolish. Our prejudice—created by culture and the common usage of modern language—asserts that "demon" is synonymous with "evil being." As we have pointed out, this is historically only a recent notion, but it is one we have to live with, so let us deal with both problems—the prejudice and the terminology—by making some comparisons.

According to classical Hermeticism, nearly any spirit of superior intelligence and power likely to appear at a conjuration would be classed as a demon. This excludes spirits of the dead, elementals, demi-gods (an unclear category) and gods. Once again, we return to Voodoo as one of the few pristine examples of this attitude still in existence. In Haiti, the spirits dealt with are called *Loa*. In Latin American Santeria and Macumba, they are referred to as *Orisha*, after the Yoruba tradition. Both these terms are usually translated as "gods," and when white European types read about Voodoo they think they are reading about the "worship" of these "gods."

In fact, the relationship to these beings is far different than what white Christian culture is accustomed to. There is direct communication and interaction. Possession is an integral part of the practice and not considered in the least

sinister. What is more, the spirits are not *quite* omniscient
or omnipotent even in their own fields. They need things
from us and as a result, deals are struck. From the point of
view of Voodoo or Macumba, the creator god is so big and
so far distant, that he has no contact with man. But other
beings, the Loa, who are pure mind but also part of the
world of nature, are not only willing to interact with man,
but need him for their own development and well being.
There are many of them and they are divided into families.
For example, there are a number of different "Erzulies":
Erzulie, Erzulie Dantor, Erzulie Ge Rouge, Erzulie Petro,
and so forth. These are not "aspects" of a single divinity,
but individual personalities given titles or names related to
their powers and place in nature. This same sort of division
occurs with the other classes of Loa, so that far from having
a pantheon of a dozen or so gods as the Romans did (at the
beginning), they deal with an entire population of spirits
that resemble the crowded ranks of the Medieval
demonologies.

For the good Christian this is a sign of primitive superstition. After all, he would say, monotheism makes more
sense, doesn't it? Some academics see monotheism as a
higher form of evolution simply because it appears to have
followed polytheism temporally. A noted exception to this
prejudice is Dr. James Hillman, the noted Jungian Analyst.

Our culture has been gradually separated over a period of
centuries from the direct individual experience of the
"supernatural." The average middle-class Christian believes
in one god because he is told to—no other reason. This is
accomplished through repetition of what constitutes "good
belief" throughout childhood, and ridicule or defamation of
"bad belief" as an adult ("those people are crackpots";
"those people sacrifice babies.") Much of this is called
"tradition."

The *Voudouist* on the other hand, believes what he experiences. True, it may be in a traditional framework that our

culture may not accept, but the *experience* is what is important. Such a person believes in spirits because he has spoken to one and been spoken to in return and has seen the spirits perform "miracles," *not* because he has to believe in this way to be a good boy. The Church "rightly" finds this an enormous threat, hence the unrelenting campaign of extermination and libel that it has waged for almost two millennia. This also explains the Church's inability to compete with Voodoo either in Haiti or Brazil, hard as it has tried.

Demons were traditionally supposed to have a kind of body. According to Agrippa and others, this is of a substance more subtle than fully physical matter—a kind of vapor or ether. This body, while freer and less imprisoned by physical boundaries than ours, is still limited by time and space, although in a different way. For example, many demons are adept at seeing the future, but so are many people. Their aid is useful, however, in influencing people and events in ways difficult or impossible for a human being.

Having bodies, they need to eat (or something similar). According to neo-Platonist and modern Voodoo they could gain sustenance from blood, flesh and, sometimes, the sex act. All of this we regard as rank superstition, but anyone who has been in a house plagued by a poltergeist knows that *something* is moving those objects and responds in an intelligent way. This at least implies a mind linked with a body *of some kind*. So Agrippa and his colleagues may have simply have been theorizing based upon observed experience rather than exercising their gullibility. Incidentally, those of you interested in the subject at all may object that poltergeists are "explained" by the subconscious violence of disturbed adolescents. Well, there were no children in the "haunted" house that was observed by Jason Black. Further, both video and audio recordings of poltergeist phenomena have been made by machines left running when there were no people present at all. While certainly we don't claim to know absolutely the causes of poltergeist phenomena, we do know that if you look at the historical data, the "disturbed adolescent" idea looks less like a valid theory and more like selective attention. (But not always. After all, if we have many of the same capacities as the alleged spirits, we must occasionally use them.)

The cultural relationship with demons has varied widely. For many, there is simple disbelief. For the modern Protestant there is hysterical fear. There is also the formal goal-oriented dealing of some of the Tibetan Tantrik sects, where communion with demons is used as a method of spiritual progress. The neo-Platonist and some Gnostics also had this attitude, as did the Renaissance magi. There is, of course, the "familiar" which can be anything from an elemental spirit of mediocre intelligence, to a sophisticated and powerful entity that has made a close alliance with a sorcerer for whatever reason. So-called "demon worship" is the treating of a particularly powerful and high ranking spirit as a kind of demi-god, giving it adoration and offerings on a regular basis in return for service, or out of fear.

Finally, there is the forbidden (in our culture) sexual relationship, the "demon lover" referred to in poetry and Gothic fiction and also more recently in the movies.

This kind of phenomenon is experienced more often in the modern world than most people realize. This is probably because anyone who has had such an encounter involuntarily is unlikely to talk about it except to his or her therapist. Who can blame them? In previous centuries, such an admission could be the first step toward the stake. In contemporary society, it's the first step toward the seventy-two hour observation cell and Thorazine.

A few cases of this kind are encountered by psychical researchers. The horror film *The Entity,* based on the novel of the same name, was taken from an actual case of a woman who was repeatedly *raped*, sometimes in front of witnesses, by an invisible being of great size, strength and odor. We have a friend who is a counselor, and sometimes deals with unorthodox or "spiritual" situations. Several years ago, he was asked to help a woman whose daughter was, in her words, "possessed." It seems the girl's brother (they were both in their early twenties) had committed suicide by hanging himself in the garage not long before, and since that time, he had been visiting her bed every night. This, he was told, was to continue an incestuous relationship that they had carried on since puberty. Apparently this was more than hysteria, since the mother claimed to have seen the ghost as well. Our friend performed an exorcism and removed the clothes that the boy had committed suicide in and the visitations ceased.

In our culture, such a relationship is grounds for panic or punishment. Since "heretic" is no longer fashionable (and we use that word deliberately), "mentally ill" is the term that has replaced it, meaning essentially the same thing or worse. There are many health care professionals in this country who consider the claim of having a psychic experience grounds for drug therapy. In fact there is a movement under way to make spirit possession and the like a "new" form of psychopathology. An erotic encounter with an spiritual being is right over the edge.

There is a parallel phenomenon that has caught the public attention. For the last thirty years or so, and especially for the last fifteen, there have been an ever-increasing number of people who claim to have been abducted by aliens. There is a great deal of controversy over this, and since we (mercifully) haven't had the experience, we won't support or deny it. The salient feature here is that a number of these people, of both genders, claim to have had sex with these beings. While most researchers in this field tend to believe that, if real, the phenomenon is extraterrestrial in nature, there are a few dissenters. The most prominent of these is

Dr. Jacques Vallee, a computer scientist and astronomer who has been investigating UFOs since the 1960's.

He claims that such encounters have been going on throughout human history, and documents his claims with chronicles going back a millennium containing accounts of people who have had lovers that they variously called *succubi*, the *Tuatha de Danaan* or fairies. He suggests that the intelligences behind these events are terrestrial and have always been with us. He also suggests that the appearance of extra-terrestrial origin is only an illusion created to give modern people something they can grasp (demons are also out of fashion), and for purposes of their own these beings want to create a new myth. We don't know what validity this idea has, but it sounds rather like the demons of the air may still be with us.

In previous times, high adepts of magic would deliberately pursue such an intimate relationship with demonic beings. The *Dakinis* of Tantrik theology are nothing less than demons, although once again, western translators tend to interpret them as gods. These *Dakinis* have an important place in the history of Tantra, particularly in Tibet. According to legend, Padmasambhava, the Indian prince who brought Tantra to Tibet in the eighth century, received his initiation from a demoness as he lay within her in a sexual embrace. This event was alleged to have occurred in a cremation ground, a not unromantic setting from the Tantrik point of view.

In all these varying cultural contexts, when one gets past the differing names and the layers of theology like varnish over an old painting, a common experience can be seen. The various demonologies and religious scaffolding are irrelevant, as are, to a certain extent, the names. We doubt very much that if we conjure, say, Astaroth, and something comes, that it is the very demon of the Mesopotamians. What matters is that the thing that responds matches the qualities that we need when we call Astaroth. And if it *is* the same being, how could we ever know? The names and sigils are important as tools for contact with, as Aleister Crowley said, "another."

The paramount utility of names and sigils is as a beacon to this hidden world from which magic draws its power. This is why traditional forms are important and still useful. Not because the standing armies of Hell literally exist (though you may believe that they do), but because when certain signs are made, and certain actions performed, it is understood by "another" what you are calling and how "it" (or they) should respond.

CHAPTER ELEVEN

The Blood Sacrifice

*On Ritual Sacrifice: I've never prescribed it, but not because
I don't believe in it. I don't know how it works, but it does.*
— Dr. Thomas Adeoye Lambo, Nigerian Psychiatrist

A word of caution: We feel that the reader should be
aware that other terms for the blood sacrifice exist and are
frequently used. However, these terms are primarily legalistic, moralistic and psychological. When these terms are
used instead of "the blood sacrifice," there is a powerful
but subtle tendency to lose the original magical-religious
significance of the blood sacrifice.

The tendency on the part of humans to interpret the past
in terms of present day ideas and values, while innovative,
has done significant damage to the magico-religious
instinct in man. In fact our technical and moral language
has taken much of the "blood" (awe) out of life, dehuman-
izing man and harming nature. Our modern scientific-ratio-
nal attitude *has* become a new religion. (See Robert Anton
Wilson's *New Inquisition*, New Falcon Publications, 1991.)

Blood itself is both a symbol of life and a sign of death.
The scientific view of the 19th century considered blood to
be the primary factor in character, ability, race and mind.
Blood lines related to reproduction and family relationships
as well as conveying rights to offspring.

The blood sacrifice refers to the shedding of blood within
a ritualistic religious context. At certain times and in certain
cultures the blood sacrifice included the ritualistic killing of

animals, adults and children. On occasion the blood sacrifice included the taking of human heads which sometimes led to the infamous "ball game."

Blood has played a significant part in the drama of human history. In the Old Testament there are numerous references to the blood sacrifices practiced by the early Hebrews. When the references of the New Testament are included there are 375 references to blood in the entire Bible.

The references to blood in the Bible are both complex and contradictory. Much of this can be resolved by employing simple ideas such as who is speaking, when a passage was written, how it is used, who is the object of discussion and what is the relationship between the "parties" involved. Sometimes the blood sacrifice is of supreme good and at others times it is of supreme evil. Frequently it is used metaphorically and the interpretation depends on whether the blood sacrifice and blood were considered good or evil, and for whom.

For the sake of exercise compare the four following passages from the bible: "And the priest shall bring it unto the altar, and wring off his head, and burn it on the altar; and the blood thereof shall be wrung out at the side of the altar" (Lev. 1:15); from Exod. 34:25, "Thou shall not offer the blood of my sacrifice with leaven; neither shall the sacrifice of the feast of the Passover be left unto morning." From Rev. 12:11, "And they overcame him by the blood of the Lamb, and by the word of their testimony; and they loved not their lives unto the death." Finally from Prov. 1:16, "For their feet run to evil, and make haste to shed blood."

Regardless, of how, when and why the ideas of blood have changed throughout the Bible it can be said that blood was a significant issue.

The famous blood sacrifice story with which most of us are familiar is that of Abraham and Isaac. As we are told

Abraham was ordered by IHVH to kill his son Isaac. Abraham is about to do this in obedience to IHVH when the Holy One tells him not to. (Some historians believe that Abraham probably did sacrifice Isaac.) Instead a covenant is made between Abraham and IHVH and a new epoch of history begins. In this case the blood sacrifice served at least two purposes: to test Abraham and to symbolize the beginning of a new epoch in Hebrew history. Other religious scholars believe that the Abraham/Isaac story simply served as a warning by God to his people not to harm others and to stop practicing the then prevalent pagan ritual of child sacrifice. We feel that this last explanation is a moralistic "wonder story."

Later we will see how the blood sacrifice has been used to initiate a new period of history. In fact many social-historians and philosophers believe that war serves this same purpose.

While the definition of the blood sacrifice at the beginning of this chapter has been used in the study of its history and origins, some writers wishing to awaken their audience to the horrors of which humans are capable have broadened the original definition of human sacrifice to include such themes as: war, abortion, reduction of welfare benefits for children, reduction of educational benefits for children, the loss of afternoon milk for children, slavery, the exploitation of natural resources, female discrimination, wife beatings, the witch hunt, homosexual persecution, child abuse, the mistreatment of elders and capital punishment. We will discuss the use, and misuse, of the meaning of the blood sacrifice later on in this chapter.

The blood sacrifice is as old as the human race. It appears that from the beginning of time humans have felt an urge to sacrifice other living things for specific religious purposes. While some researchers have attempted to explain away some blood sacrifices (cannibalism) as a reaction to hunger or as a form of population control, their reductionist explanations have been found wanting. (See below for a similar "comforting" explanation for alcohol use amongst primitives.) For example, some tribes have been found to increase their blood sacrifices during harvest and upon completing a successful hunt.

The desire to find comforting explanations for this common human behavior can't simply be satisfied by hypothesizing a lack of adequate protein sources, although in some cases of mass cannibalism, at times this might also be true. However, even in cannibalism the consumption of blood or body parts can have significant religious and magical proprieties. Some research has shown that certain groups believed that cannibalism was the supreme way of experiencing communion with the Gods. In this sense the people were saying, what God can do we can also do—kill.

The number of reasons given for why people perform the blood sacrifice can boggle the mind. We will explore many of them throughout this chapter as well as investigate some of the rituals themselves. However, before exploring these topics we should warn the reader that the blood sacrifice is still practiced today by many millions of people in the civilized world.

Many of us are familiar with Count Dracula's famous saying, "the blood is the life." This quote, which comes from the Bible (Deut. 12:23), often brings laughter and at the same time stirs other and possibly more primordial feelings. The horror associated with the blood sacrifice seems universal within certain social classes, particularly the white middle class, but the simple feeling of horror doesn't mean that revulsion and aversion have won out, even within these groups. The horror of the blood sacrifice covers a deeper feeling, the one of participating in a cosmic event—uniting man with God as well as the beasts through the medium of death and blood.

I KILLED A BEAST & DRANK OF ITS BLOOD

From a modern point of view the hands on killing of animals, whether by hunting or sacrifice, is frowned upon. During other times—possibly more human and holy times—there was a dynamic relationship between the killing of animals and man. During these times the animal was really the "other." Man knew himself through this relationship with the animals he hunted and worshipped. Man's relationship with animals gave him a profound sense of his own body and identity.

The animal was sacred, respected for his powers and abilities and in this sense man was sacred. To kill an animal with one's hands was a holy act. Today we simply keep animals as pets, experiment on them in laboratories, have them star in cartoons and eat them after they have been processed. They are no longer sacred and neither are we.

For modern man everything is simply a resource. If asked: "a resource for what?" the answer is: "for the service of mankind."

Even humans are thought of as resources: many governments and corporations have "Departments of Human Resources." We have generalized our attitudes about animals to ourselves. Descartes' notion that animals are "machines" without a soul has become a reality not only for animals but for ourselves.

SACRIFICE & THE SCAPEGOAT

Unusual or frightening human behavior can usually be classified into three causative categories: (1) sin against deity, (2) crime against king and, most recently (3) insanity. The sin model places the priest between the sinner and the community; the crime model places the detective and the courts between the criminal and the community; and the insanity (medical) model places the psychiatrist and the asylum between the community and the insane person.

The primary purpose of these causative explanations is to relieve the anxiety that deviant behavior causes in the "mind" of the community. By placing a force or a group of people between the alleged anxiety-causing agent and the community, people seem to feel temporarily relieved and protected. When one explanation doesn't work, say, for example, insanity (which was popular in the 60's and 70's), then sin or crime (which was popular in 80's and 90's) rushes in as a substitute. The funny thing about all of this is that it is passed off as scientific. While these causative models seem to relieve tension and concern by allowing people to label events, these explanations in no way have scientific status simply because they relieve tension.

Another example of pseudo-science is the application of the Western tension reduction model which claims to explain drinking behavior. This model has been applied to primitive and ancient cultures and much like the blood sacrifice explanation is reductive and false. The idea that primitives simply drank to reduce tension surrounding food scarcity is contradicted by the fact that more drinking took place in times of plenty than in times of scarcity. Again, our modern view sees ancient and primitive behavior from our "superior" model of the universe and attribute to others our psychology and morality—or lack of it.

Most often these causative explanations are simply placebos for the "minds" of anxious and fearful people. Unfortunately, the people we rely on most (authorities) have the most to lose by honesty and straightforwardness.

When a civilization can no longer cope with change and anxiety it simply invents or re-invents explanations to attempt to put the population at rest. Explanations for behaviors which cause fear in the populace is often trendy, like anything else in our modern culture. Often these trends are marketed by the media through scare tactics, selective perception and retrospective examples.

OUR MODERN DAY WITCH HUNTS

In our modern day witch hunts Satanism has been resurrected as one of the causes of deviant behavior. (Other causes for the failure of this civilization include: drugs, alcohol, pornography, homosexuality, promiscuity, paganism...) Satanism has been viewed as sin, as a crime and most recently as a pathology. Thus, the priest, the cop and the psychiatrist have all been given the job of protecting the community. For example Satanism as sin has been "combated" by "Picketing 7-Elevens" for selling "pornography."

Satanism as crime has been depicted in novel, TV and motion pictures. Child abuse and incest have been connected with Satanic cults.

Satanism as insanity is now a hot topic in the psychiatric community to the extent that it has been suggested that new diagnostic categories be established for such things as Satanic possession.

When anxiety levels are high—such as they are now—more bizarre explanations are required. Today it is the association of Satanism with most everything. Drugs and Satanism, sex and Satanism, AIDS and Satanism, incest and Satanism, and the list goes on.

Before we go any further it is important to forge in the reader's mind that the blood sacrifice has nothing to do with the Devil or Satan. The association of Satanism with the blood sacrifice is a creation of the Christian Church that wished to have a complete monopoly on practicing this ancient ritual.

It is often ignored, however, that Jesus sacrificed his real body and blood in order for the Eucharist to have its spiritual significance. In other words, while the bread and the wine are symbolic of the body of Christ, real blood was shed to make this ritual significant for the human mind. At the base of the Christian belief system is the notion that the love of and for Christ will triumph over the human desire to "make" the blood sacrifice. The implications of this notion are staggering when you begin to dwell on them. One implication is that Christian "love" is powerful enough to do away with paganism entirely and to reduce the desire to sacrifice to a simple mental construct. It is advertised that Christ paid for the world's sin by his willingness to shed his blood for mankind. Christ's sacrifice was also seen as the defeat of Satan. Coupled with this defeat was the assigning of the term "evil" to anyone who would compete with the Church's practice of the blood sacrifice.

Even today in Africa, the Massai of Kenya and Tanzania, although nominally Christian, practice the blood sacrifice. This ritual is a major and important part of their tradition and way of life. They offer these sacrifices to their "one true God" *Enkai*. Although religious and church officials are aware of these activities, there is little they can do to stop them. The Christian clergy attempts to make inroads on this behavior by declaring certain blood sacrifices unacceptable while allowing the Massai to continue with others. The Christians justify this by finding similarities between Biblical scriptures and the Massai blood sacrifices which the Christians tolerate—for the time being.

MODELS OF THE BLOOD SACRIFICE

It is believed by many who practice the blood sacrifice ritual that "in the beginning" there was primeval chaos and disorder. Chaos was harmonized through a sacred killing event creating Order. This view rivals the common belief that the blood sacrifice is simply a gift to the Gods. The "Order out of Chaos" model establishes days of celebrations or holidays when the original blood sacrifice is reenacted. The distinction between the celebration of an event and a gift is the crucial difference for these two models of the blood sacrifice.

Another more practical model is the "Good/times–Bad/times" model which doesn't necessarily take into account the idea of a gift or even a celebration. For convenience sake we have called chaos "the bad times" and order "the good times." This makes for a simple four-fold model which will categorize most types of blood sacrifice.

Good Times	Bad Times
a. Bring on the good times.	c. To get rid of a bad condition.
b. Prevent the good times from departing	d. Change the bad times to good times

In situation (a) a person or tribe simply wishes to bring on a fortuitous event, say a successful harvest. Nothing bad is going on, but in order to insure the crop a blood sacrifice ritual is performed.

In situation (b) the tribe is enjoying a good harvest and the tribe insures its continuation by performing a blood sacrifice.

In situation (c) the tribe is experiencing a bad condition which they simply wish to remove. Everything else is going fine.

In situation (d) the tribe is experiencing bad times which they not only wish to remove but change to good times.

A gift to a higher power is different in kind from taking an active part in influencing the Universe in your favor. The gift notion is more passive and appeasing while the "influencing model" is more active and rebellious from our modern point of view.

While the three models of sacrifice—gifts to the Gods, celebrating a primal event (or initiating a new beginning) and influencing the forces of the universe—convey separate principles, in practice these three models are often expressed in mixed forms. An example of a mixed model is the killing of a person so he may be a messenger to a God.

The person sacrificed serves as a gift, an influence and, if the ritual is done at a sacred time, a celebration.

SOCIO-POLITICAL ASPECTS OF THE "BLOOD SACRIFICE"

The idea of initiating a new epoch by blood sacrifice is not new. For example, the creation myth surrounding Ouranos and Gaia focuses on the children of earth being trapped by the sexual embrace of the Sky and Earth. To free her children Gaia makes a sickle and gives it to Kronos her son. Kronos (not the same as Chronos although frequently interchanged with the father of Time) castrates his father putting an end to the union of Sky and Earth. Ouranos' blood falls to earth and from these drops of blood the twelve Titans and Titanesses are created. The blood sacrifice put an end to the era of Ouranos who kept his children prisoners of earth. On the other hand Kronos ate his children.

The idea of killing masses of people in the name of a deity or a new era doesn't exist only in myth nor in foreign countries. In early America our ancestors had little difficulty in reconciling their idealism with the neglect and slaughter of hundreds of thousands of Indians, the keeping of millions of slaves and looting the land. The Nazis also practiced similar rituals.

It is interesting to note that the religions of both the American Indians and the Negro slaves were eroded by the white Christian "demons." When information such as this or information about the Inquisition or the Vietnam War is presented to those who tacitly uphold Christian and American idealism they remain silent. They often justify the actions of their forefathers, or state that "those things happened in the past." However, they forget to mention how long it takes for the present to become the past.

The idea of an American *volk* is not much different from other ideas about a chosen people. Chosen people (including the Nazis) always have the right to perform blood sacrifices. The method of reconciliation is always a process of myth making and fictionalizing. Those sacrificed, in this way, are always less—inferior—not human—not "like us." This is very similar to Reagan's notion of the "evil empire"—the Russian communist looting and raping of American business.

Hitler had similar ideas about the Jews. He had little difficulty conveying the idea and meaning of blood to his people. Cleansing by blood sacrifice, while not in the spirit of what we think of as religious ritual, is nonetheless a method that civilizations have often found useful.

The Puritans in England had little difficulty killing thousands of witches to cleanse their holy land of Satan. Some researchers have estimated that over the 300-400 years of the witch hunt a minimum of a million witches (mostly older females) were sacrificed for Christendom. Other estimates go from 3-4 million, all the way up to 10 million.

The idea that the chosen have the right to perform the blood sacrifice is well expressed by feminist writers. For example one researcher has stated:

> ...that doing blood sacrifice enables participants to constitute and maintain 'eternal' lines of patrilineal descent in which membership is made known not by birth or begetting...but by rights to participate in sacrifices. (Jay, 1981)

Jay emphasizes in her work that the chosen are male. Her analysis of the blood sacrifice differs from others in that she doesn't focus on what the ritual means but rather on what the ritual does.

Although those who have "rights" to kill others require that they exercise their "rights" in order to keep them, the feminist explanation doesn't in our view explain the fascination and horror associated with the blood sacrifice. Some researchers feel that the horror which surrounds the blood sacrifice simply represents one side of the contradictory attitude toward life—human life is sacred but it is also profane. The valuelessness of human life is normally hidden from daily sight—that is, of course, unless you look for it. During times of great human destruction the valuelessness of human life is readily and easily expressed. Every individual requires to believe that his life is of value and the world is safe. The blood sacrifice is a constant reminder that something must be given up, someone must be sacrificed in order for value and order to be guaranteed. Who this someone is breeds horror in the mind of men. Everyday this unknown, unnamed someone is sacrificed. Tomorrow it might even be me or for that matter you.

THE PRACTICE OF THE BLOOD SACRIFICE

The extent to which the blood sacrifice was practiced is quite large. In fact the types of people and the details of the various sacrifices would require volumes. Some examples from different parts of the world include:

Abraham "kills" Isaac to create a new orientation for the Hebrews. In Greek mythology Agamemnon kills his daughter Iphigenia so the winds can carry the Greek ships to rescue Helen in Troy. The idol god *Molek* cult sacrificed children by fire. The Germans had a covenant with their gods which demanded not only animal and human sacrifices but supported sacrifices for victories over their enemies and sacrifices for funerals.

It is believed by some scholars that human sacrifices were still being carried out publicly in Europe in the early eighth century. This argues against the Christian belief that paganism was mostly extinct by that time.

The early Egyptians, Chinese, Japanese and Koreans practiced the "following in death" sacrifice. Slaves, wives and children accompanied their husbands in death. *Suttee* is still practiced openly in parts of India.

While it was not usually a high priority for the British to intervene with the religious practices of their colonial subjects, they expended a great amount of effort to eliminate the sacrificial habits of the Khond tribe of Africa. There is strong evidence to suggest that the ancient Etruscans carried out extensive human sacrifice. Evidence indicates that as a component of their blood sacrifice the men dressed up as wolves. Some researchers argue that this is an indication of an Egyptian influence on their rites.

It is well documented that the Phoenicians of Carthage carried out rituals of sacrificing their own children in order to get the Gods to grant them favors. It appears that the idea of killing one's own children was more horrifying to the other peoples of the time than killing someone else's children, which of course many of their neighbors practiced.

Many researchers believe that the Greeks carried out the "following in death" sacrifice as well as numerous other types of sacrifices. Even the Gods of the Homeric epics are deeply connected with human sacrifice as well as other forms of violence. On the other hand some researchers into the blood sacrifice feel that the evidence for the Greeks involvement with the blood sacrifice is inconclusive. Many people have a difficult time connecting the beauty of the Greek civilization with the idea of child and human sacrifice. Of course the Romans had their own versions of this ancient ritual.

The Hawaiians, Maoris and many other Polynesian tribes were deemed guilty of sin by the Christians not only for their relative sexual freedom but because of their involvement with the blood sacrifice.

The Hawaiians also are rumored to have had an unnerving habit of ritually killing and dining on certain of their rivals or enemies. King Kamehameha killed Captain Cook after a diplomatic *faux pas*, and is said to have eaten Cook's heart to absorb his *virtu*. This was not an act of cannibalism as we usually think of it. Kamehameha was attempting to absorb Cook's power just as a spirit would have been believed to absorb the power of a sacrifice. This justification did little to comfort Cook's crew.

During the great Viking age of Scandinavia, legend has it that humans were sacrificed to Odin in order to defend their universe against "chaos." They would also assimilate the wisdom of their victims by drinking their blood.

Of course we are all familiar with the Aztecs and Mayans and their preoccupation with human sacrifice.

Last but not least are the Americas where many forms of the blood sacrifice were and are practiced among native cultures.

What we have presented above should give the reader a small taste of the prevalence of the blood sacrifice.

THEORIES ABOUT THE BLOOD SACRIFICE

There are many theories about why humans practiced and practice the blood sacrifice: obedience to God(s), obedience to earthly rulers, to demonstrate faith, to express hope, to signify a new beginning, to gain favors from God(s), to assure an event, to prevent an event from occurring, to send a messenger to God(s), to feed mother earth, to commune with God(s) and to celebrate an event or period of time.

The theories presented above are primal and organic. These are rivaled by more "modern" speculations which are rationalistic, psychoanalytical, psychological and socio-anthropological-political theories.

For example, one political-social theory posits that the power to perform the blood sacrifice stabilizes the community as well as assuring the status quo of the prevailing power structure. Another claims that cannibalism was simply a form of population control.

One psychoanalytic theory holds that the blood sacrifice was simply a "projection of human aggression against deities," (Bergmann, 1990). This theorist also believes that

when an individual inhibits a desire in favor of the authority of the father (the superego) there is a feeling of
sacrifice. From this theory we speculate that the need to
sacrifice is believed to be satisfied by this mental operation.
This type of thinking is similar to the Christian notion
mentioned earlier that Christian "love" can take the place
for the need to "make" sacrifice.

It appears that the Jews were a little ahead of the Christians when they "outlawed" aspects of the blood sacrifice
only to replace it with circumcision and the prohibition
against drinking blood. The prohibition against drinking
blood is so strong for the Jews that they slaughter and
process meat in such a way as to remove from it as much
blood as possible. Another aspect of the Jewish slaughter
ritual is that blessings are said over the animal by a Rabbi.
The combination of draining away the blood and saying a
blessing is inherently more organic and is closer to fulfilling the need for "making" a blood sacrifice than simple
Christian "love" or making a sacrifice to the super-ego
(father, the state, or the tribal chief).

Some other theories regarding the nature of the blood
sacrifice are a mixture of psychoanalysis, politics and soci-
ology. One, for example, holds that the child sacrifice is
simply the projection of evil or unwanted characteristics
onto the child. This allows the adult to perform the sacrifice, whether it is murder or other forms of child abuse.
This same theory has been applied to the persecution of
dark races as well as to women. This theory of the projection of evil, combined with the theory that the blood sacrifice against children is payment for past sins of adults, may
hold some observational truth. But in our view it is more a
pathological reaction against the repressive mechanisms
which made the blood sacrifice a moral issue.

The "making" of the blood sacrifice is both organic and
instinctual; and the methods used to suppress individuals
from partaking in the blood sacrifice is a "causative" factor

in its severe pathological manifestation. Modern wars, which do not even allow people to see or touch each other when they kill, will in our view, lead to further pathological manifestations of the need to "make" blood sacrifice in more devastating forms.

Other theorists argue that males perform the majority of blood sacrifices due to some sort of envy toward women— who perform a blood sacrifice on a monthly basis. Frequently conjoined with this theory is the idea that females are simply the objects of male rage and violence because they were aware of how life was created. These theorists seem to forget that women are just as human as men and they have a long history of human sacrifice. Of course these theorists then argue that women's blood sacrifice is simply displaced aggression. Again, these theorists seem to forget the Goddess Kali. When such issues are brought up they usually respond by stating that Kali worship is primitive compared to our civilization.

Others posit oral aggressive drives as the basis for blood sacrifice. They believe that such terms as "oral aggression" *explain* the blood sacrifice rather than simply describing a behavior associated with it.

Still others believe that the people who have performed blood sacrifices are perpetrators and the creature sacrificed is simply a victim. These theorists often conclude that the "perpetrator" achieves a feeling of omnipotence by performing the sacrifice. In this context the religious qualities of the blood sacrifice have been replaced by moralistic and legalistic ones.

While there is no doubt some truth—at the level of description—in all these theories, a description can never be assumed to be a cause. The primitive idea that labeling and description provides one with a causative explanation tells us more about the operations of the human mind then it tells us about the blood sacrifice.

More developmental and sociological theorists argue that the blood sacrifice is simply a stage in cultural evolution in which group anxieties were dealt with through public ritual. (Our modern notion of capital punishment may be a "development" of the blood sacrifice.) Over time the blood ritual is replaced by political and religious institutions. This argument at least supports the idea that there are deeper needs which the blood sacrifice fulfills. The blood ritual is not simply aggression against deities or women. We have at times presented this argument to individuals who do not have an anthropological sense of the development of cultural institutions. Usually they feel upset by the idea that "their" civilization is only a few steps ahead of the blood sacrifice. Instead of using the term blood sacrifice these individuals prefer such terms as homicide or murder. Legalistic terms as well as those that "diagnose" the blood sacrifice as psychopathology miss the point that the blood sacrifice is organic to man.

Some researchers see the abolition of the blood sacrifice as a victory for mankind. They feel that while humans have a desire to perform the blood sacrifice they have an almost equal desire not to practice it. They see many religious holidays as an expression of the victory over the blood sacrifice. For example, one researcher sees the Jewish holiday of Hanukkah as a profound expression of the "sun's victory over darkness" and the Jewish repression of the blood sacrifice. Some of these ideas might be classed as sublimation theories.

The attempt to historize and psychologize the blood sacrifice gives us a profound opportunity to see how modern thoughts about organic and archaic processes can be used to separate ourselves from our primal origins. This act of reinterpretation to separate ourselves from our own past, though highly imaginative, can also cause great harm. For example, the destructive behavior shown toward the earth is one result of separating ourselves from our primordial origins. Our scientific and consumer ethic, though providing many benefits, has cost us as well.

THE HORROR OF BLOOD.
FINDING A LOGICAL SUBSTITUTE.
THE BLOODY MARY HOAX

While the drink "bloody Mary" no doubt refers to the murdering queen, the popularity of the drink may also have something to do with a substitute for the blood sacrifice. While true or not we have had some fun mentioning this idea to devotees of this drink.

Food, minor acts of blood sacrifice (for example, circumcision), liquor, special feasts and rituals have all served to take the place of the blood sacrifice. Regardless of the form of the sacrifice from simply killing an animal to decapitating a human and eating his body and drinking his blood—overt practice of the blood sacrifice has all but disappeared from the modern world.

The exceptions include pathological killers such as Shawcross, who ate the body parts of some of his prostitute victims, and heroic fictional cannibals such as Hannibal Lecter, who was obsessed with human flesh. The blood sacrifice has all but left us in the Western-White-Christian world. Or has it?

Today in America millions of people are performing the blood sacrifice using real blood instead of wine or incense sticks. This group is known as Santeria. A combination of ancient African religion and Christian symbolism, these modern day practitioners are sacrificing animals within the context of their religious belief system. While animal sacrifice is illegal—except when defined as butchery for food in licensed establishments and for animal experimentation—the growing group of Santeria has all but ignored the laws which restrict them from practicing their religion. It is estimated that their are five million devoted followers of Santeria in the United States alone.

THE USE OF THE BLOOD SACRIFICE IN MAGIC

Magic is the socially unauthorized use of the will and imagination to partake in the powers of the universe. According to most western religionists magic is fundamentally Satanic and evil. Most academics usually view magic from a developmental point of view when they study primitive cultures. Psychologists often see magic as pathological and regressive, though many do not view religion in the same way.

Some sociologists see magic's reemergence as a warning sign that a civilization is entering a crisis period. But while magic may signal that our culture is in "trouble" it doesn't mean that magic is *only* a signal for cultures in trouble. Magic existed long before sociologists and served man more faithfully than these pseudo-scientific explanations about the *meaning* of magic.

Modern people often ignore the psychological importance of the magical gesture. Or do they?

In fact the brain is structured in such a way that events which follow each other or look similar are assumed to be connected or causative. It has taken humans thousands of years to see, even if for a moment, cause and effect differently. Yet, there is a reason why events which follow each other or are similar are seen as connected. The human brain knows that "cause" is less important than survival. If you see "a many spotted thing" in the jungle, don't wait. Run in the opposite direction.

While our public image is rational, scientific and religious our actual day-to-day experience is magical. We have strong feelings about certain things like blood, nude bodies, our genitals, birth, death, food and hair. Each of us have mini-cosmologies built around ourselves and family. Many of us think in terms of luck or chance rather than cause and effect. Most of us are so deeply affected by our developmental circumstances that we only give lip service to rationality, logic and religious beliefs. In some non-verbal way all of us sense how the world really works. Most of us ignore the reality of death believing, especially if we are young, that we are personally immune from death, ill fortune and disease.

How many of us are not fascinated by the magical powers we see portrayed in today's occult and science fiction movies? We all have heroes who we believe have strange and unusual qualities that we would like to have. And if the truth be known, most of us perform mini-gestures such as counting, concentrating, praying, avoiding certain situations, etc., to affect our personal lives. We all have beliefs and thoughts which defy rationality and common sense.

The primary differences between practicing magicians and those who practices magic automatically are knowledge and form. Those who practice ritual to affect themselves and the universe have both background and technique to aid them in their manipulations. These methods range from simple incantations to elaborate spectacular ceremonies, some of which include actual blood sacrifices or substitutes like incense, sexual fluids and wine.

One purpose of the blood sacrifice is to "fixate" the mind. What we mean by "fixate" is to energize it, to shock it into a different plane of reality. Physiologically we respond with increases in hormonal output and we feel an arousal which some people have likened to terror. The sacrifice of the animal or its substitute opens, as some occultists have said, a "corridor" to the universe.

In some Voodoo rituals insects are used to symbolize an enemy and the insect is destroyed or bound. In other rituals chickens, doves, finches, frogs, or rats are used to create the power necessary to "cause" the desired effect.

From a more materialistic point of view, the sacrifice of flesh and blood isn't for symbolic purposes at all. In this view, which is the view of most of the Voodoo religions (Voodoo, Macumba, Santeria) the sacrifice literally releases energy which "feeds" an "objective" spirit entity. This spirit then has the power (as well as the inclination) to affect the world in the way the sorcerer desires. This is most likely the way the *Bocors* or *Santeros* themselves would explain the practice, and it dispenses with some of the more absurd academic "explanations" cited above.

The three Grimoires presented in this book all include animal sacrifice in their rituals. Due largely to remarks by Eliphas Levi and A.E. Waite made in the last century, the blood sacrifices in these books are supposed to be a sign of the blackest depravity. Most suburban practitioners of magic or "witchcraft " are quick to agree.

But wait.

What is it that is sacrificed in these rituals? Chicken and sheep and goats. What was it that had to be sacrificed by every household every day for lunch before the invention of the ice box? Chicken and sheep and goats. Almost all of us over the age of twelve had Grandmothers or Great-Grandmothers who routinely bought live fowl at the market (even in the city) killed it, plucked it and cooked it for the kids. These housewives were hardly guilty of a satanic act.

These animals are killed by the millions in modern slaughterhouses in a grotesquely slow and inhumane way— far slower than at the hands of a *Santero*, a magician or a housewife.

Chickens are placed on a conveyor and passed through a machine that tears off their beaks to keep them quiet and less violent while they wait to die. Cattle are herded with an electric prod down a ramp so steep that their legs are often broken before they reach the bottom. They are then supposed to be killed by a single blow or shot to the head. In practice, they only die sometimes. Dead or not, a hook and chain is passed through their flesh, and they are towed by a tractor to a heap of other helpless and dying animals to bleat out their last minutes or hours. Many of the same people who buy the processed product of this pain in a suburban supermarket would run for the police if a magician killed a chicken quickly and cleanly in a ritual act, even if he ate it for dinner later. The only difference between the tortuous legal act and the painless "criminal" act is the non-Christian ritual aspect, an element that is more metaphysical and political than real.

THE SOCIAL TRANSMUTATION OF THE BLOOD SACRIFICE

Recently, on a national news broadcast, there was a segment taped in New York. The video showed ranks of cages containing sheep and chickens, with NYPD officers standing with military solemnity in front of them. The police, the commentator informed us, had just "rescued" these animals. Not from torture or some other form of lingering abuse, but from a place where a major Santeria festival was about to be celebrated. What was to be the fate of these *livestock* animals? They would be killed expertly and quickly by a *Santero*, the blood given to the *Orishas* as a gift, and most likely (depending on the ritual) the animals would be cooked and eaten that same evening by the men women and children at the celebration.

Watching this report (similar to ones New Yorkers must have seen dozens of times) one wonders if the animals would have been confiscated or the *Santeros* arrested if they were just going to have them for dinner? The answer: if they had just been preparing a large community dinner "from scratch" they might have gotten a citation. The reason for the arrests, confiscation and nationwide publicity was the religion element *only*.

As stated earlier, the process of slaughtering livestock in a kosher fashion involves the draining of the blood while a rabbi pronounces a blessing. This, *by definition*, is ritual animal sacrifice, and if it did not occur hundreds of times a day there would be no kosher meat. Are the participants in these (according to Waite and Levi and modern law enforcement) "satanic" rituals arrested? Are the animals "rescued"?

Of course not. The issue never arises.

This is religious bigotry pure and simple. While legally we are a secular society, culturally we have a monolithic, even fascist religious influence programmed into the bulk of the white middle class. This makes enormous numbers of people rigidly locked into a repressed, fearful and highly artificial world view, and their only option in reacting to something alien is some form of violence. If a good excuse for this doesn't legitimately exist, one is fabricated. The revival of interest in magic that occurred thirty years ago in Western culture produced shock waves of profound emotional disturbance in this "hysterical" underclass. There was no legal, legitimate reason to attack this cultural change, so they invented one: the Satanist Conspiracy. Since the blood sacrifice in a religious context is exactly the sort of deep instinctual experience that terrifies them, they created the absurd myth of thousands of sacrificed children. This gives the rationale to use the police (physical force) to combat the new rival religious view. Since many police are members of this "hysterical underclass" and share their paranoid fears and repressions, there is no difficulty in this.

There is another distorting element to their behavior. Jason Black grew up in the Midwest, in a largely Protestant community with a noticeable fundamentalist presence. What he observed in people who never divorced themselves from this influence was a thin layer of "respectable" behavior covering a reservoir of denied rage, sadism and masochism. This was manifested as physical and mental abuse within families which was either justified in Biblical terms or ignored ("it didn't happen.") This was, and is, so endemic that it constitutes normalcy for much of society. From having spent the first half of his life around such people, he personally suspects that the "child sacrifice" panic is a manifestation of what such perpetually angry and frightened people would, in their deepest hearts, like to do themselves. In other words, the mythical world organization of Satanists is a manifestation of their alter egos, their instinctual selves. It is no wonder that one of the basic tenets of their religion(s) is that only "Jesus" can save a man from being depraved and evil. It isn't true for the world at large, but it certainly must seem so when they look in the mirror.

Only last week there was one of the almost endless talk shows on the subject of "satanic survivors," people who "suddenly" remember being raised in a murderous diabolical cult. In this particular instance, it was two young people in their twenties and their mother.

According to their story, the father (not on the show) had the children, when small, drug the mother (a registered nurse) *every night*, and have them help him in "satanic ceremonies" that included "hundreds" of human sacrifices. None of these, of course, have ever been discovered. The "drugged" mother was so pathological that it was obvious to any intelligent viewer, and it was casually mentioned in passing, that the children both had multiple personalities. Nothing much was made of either of these facts by the host. No professional evaluation was made on the kind of background (aside from Satanism of course) that might have produced such symptoms, and the mother was unable to explain coherently why she, a registered nurse, never noticed that she was being drugged to unconsciousness every night for several years.

We hardly need to add that these people were fundamentalist Christians who had in their church a ready-made support structure for this kind of delusion, as well as help to deny any mental health problems embedded in their "Christian family." And what of the sinister Satanist who forced his children to participate in hundreds of human sacrifices? He's a mail carrier in the Midwest, who, it is safe to say, is staying as far away from his loving family as possible.

All this nonsense is the result of the need to label something threatening so we can kill it. In magic, the first step toward controlling a force or intelligence is to learn its name. This is also one of the principle functions of sacrifice. An animal or thing is baptized as the enemy and then destroyed.

In this new urban myth there is a two-fold function. First, the child abuse and brutality that is endemic in our culture—especially, as any experienced therapist will tell you, in fundamentalist subcultures—is given an alien label. Good Christians *can't* abuse their children to the point where they become schizophrenic, so these people must be Satanists. Few, if any Christians see the Christian world view as possessing one iota of psychopathology or being anti-life. The need to deny that their only source of comfort and identity is the very thing that has destroyed them is stronger than any facts or rational thought. Hence, in some people, childhood abuse is "forgotten." They need to ignore that brutality is brutality, and putting a foreign name on it doesn't change the results of the experience. Childhood abuse is common in all aspects of our culture, to the point where it is "normal," and confronting that simple fact seems an impossible task for many.

The second function is political. In the West, the power of the church has been on a downhill slide for two hundred years. Especially since the end of the second world war, the population at large has been drifting away from traditional religion (Christianity). For the first time in four hundred years there are actually competing religions, not to mention scientific knowledge, that threaten Christian domination. The kind of rage, anxiety and paranoia that this produces in a half-educated population weaned on "one god" and "one true religion" (which adds up to "one group in power") has to be experienced to be appreciated. Anything not part of the group is labeled as dangerous or criminal, no matter how innocuous. One woman (Lutheran) from Jason Black's home town told him she thought that meditation caused demonic possession. The solution to this dilemma? A new witch-hunt. The myth of the Satanic Network gives these people a reason to exterminate the emerging new social reality. Those familiar with the pathology evident in the old witch trials have already drawn comparisons.

What has all this to do with the subject of the blood sacrifice? The proponents of the new paradigm are given the role of scapegoat. The fundamentalists feel sure, even when they don't verbalize it, that the elimination of the new religions will "make everything all right again," the way *It Used To Be*. This kind of reaction is absolutely typical of a social structure in decay, in the process of being replaced by what we hypothesize to be a Magical-Scientific one.

Occult and religious movements are by no means the only targets for this kind of scapegoating. Any group that was once a "designated victim," that could be abused by anyone with impunity, and which is now coming into power, becomes a target.

Racial and sexual minorities are in the same position. Before the mid 1960's, one could amuse oneself by beating a "kike," "nigger" or a "fag" with a baseball bat on a Saturday night, and the odds are that no report would even be filed with the authorities. That was viewed (by both sides) as the order of things and wasn't a social issue. Now, with gays and blacks asserting their right to live the way they please and have political and economic clout, they are seen as the same kind of threat as the "Satanic Network," and for the same reasons. The power to subjugate someone physically and economically is one of the most fundamental forms of asserting social rank. Terrible as it sounds, there is a sizable population in our culture who feel a

personal loss of self-esteem because they can no longer
assault a black or homosexual or, for that matter, a woman
without being arrested. On a recent news program a hidden
camera captured the arrest of a Houston man after he
attacked an undercover officer. He kept asking why he was
being arrested. "I told you I was sorry," he said. "I thought
you was a damn queer!"

This threatened class of people has given rise to the
revival of Ku Klux Klan type secret societies, dedicated to
the extermination (sacrifice) of the threatening organism.

What is interesting from the point of view of the magician, is that this kind of mass hysteria and violence is both
triggered and *controlled* by the use of symbols. As both
Hitler and the Renaissance magi knew well, simply expos-
ing the uninitiated mob to certain carefully chosen images
and words—*empty in themselves*—can create fear, adoration or violence.

It is this fundamental violent force in our organisms that
is roused and manipulated by magical techniques. It is the
fact that these techniques work that make them so frightening to the average man. The blood sacrifice is universal. It
occurs in every culture without exception. This, like the
basic activities of shamanism, seems to be biological,
something mankind is programmed with.

Those cultures, like our own, that deny the place of the
sacrifice in their psychology and religion must sublimate it
in some way. A society can be judged by the substitute they
select for the sacrificial beast.

In our culture, as has been pointed out, it seems to be
people—destroyed and slaughtered under the disguise of
"moral necessity."

The regressive longings "for the good old days" which
never existed, is finding its way into every aspect of human
life. Everyone is becoming suspect of violating the values
and morals of Christendom. In times of collapsed reason,
the rights of the individual are re-framed as simple asser-

tions and consensus reality. People are frightened and hence frightening. Feeling threatened they are willing to sacrifice just about anyone or anything for relief. Instead of chickens, it is groups of people who are different in some way from the fictitious norm. Not only are women and children victims, but the rebellion against the male dominance as practiced by the hypocrites of Christianity has taken on a "new" perversion of its own.

The patriarchy, in order to protect its privileged position are sacrificing lesser males to the beast of conformity. For example, men are "guilty" of date rape simply because they say that "unless we have sex I won't date you anymore." Some sociologists and psychologists see this simple negotiation strategy as exploitive and violent—some believe it is deserving of punishment.

Sexual behavior is again becoming an issue, not simply because of AIDS but because of the need of a culprit. New classes of people are being invented. They are labeled as victims and perpetrators. Everyone is a potential perpetrator until proven a victim. For example some individuals in power support laws and administrative rules that does away with due process as well as the statue of limitations on certain newly defined "crimes." Currently it is a crime for a therapist to have sex with a former patient for a designated number of years after therapy is terminated. One gentlemen has gone so far as to propose making this intervening period "forever."

In other cases leaders of sovereign countries are kidnapped or murdered because they violate our Christian-Judaic world view and "logic."

In our view, the witch hunts of today will expand to the point where sooner or later everybody will have to be seen as an enemy of the collapsing Church and State. Thus, the blood sacrifice may become the only means by which the Church and State maintain their power.

PART II

PRACTICE

Satan

Transformed from Pagan God to Rebel Angel

Lucifer
As described in *The Grimorium Verum*

Astaroth
According to *The Grimorium Verum*

He is the "Black Man" said to preside over the witch's sabbath. Traditionally a Lord of perverse eroticism.

Beelzebuth
According to *The Grimorium Verum*

The fly on the throne is a reference to his title
"Lord of the Flies."

Pope Honorius

An imaginary portrait showing the blessing and cursing
powers of the Church.

A possible altar arrangement using an image, for the
contemplative or Tantrik style of evocation. Includes
libation, sigils, magical weapons and divinatory tools.

Possible arrangement for a sex magick ritual.
The sign on the banner is Aleister Crowley's
"Sun and Moon Conjoined"
or the erotic uniting of opposite principles.

"Magical Figures"

From *The Constitution of Honorius*.
Based on a seventeenth century original.

CHAPTER TWELVE

Introduction To The Grimoires

Important note: The following three Grimoires contain references to the religious sacrifice of animals. These are included for historical purposes only and are not intended for use. Other more modern and legal sacrifices can be used or invented by the practitioner.

The rituals that follow were taken from three books: *The Grimorium Verum, The Grand Grimoire* and *The Constitution of Honorius*. They have been edited by the authors in order to make them more sensible and usable by the person so inclined. In the particular case of *The Grand Grimoire* it has been drastically edited and adapted to modern practice so that it is essentially a new document.

The Grimorium Verum has been edited of some absurd and archaic material of no use to the magician (for example a spell for teleporting garters), but is essentially the original document.

The Constitution of Honorius has been greatly expanded to include rituals and psalms only referred to in the original version. This is so that the serious practitioner may use this ritual without having to access a public library.

All of the rituals that follow are mutually compatible and portions of one can be used within the framework of another at the practitioners discretion.

The editors have selected the psalms in *The Constitution of Honorius* for their meaning and poetic power. In the original version, the psalms were part of a devotional practice still used by Catholic and Episcopal Priests and change on a monthly basis. The psalms selected here may be used in whole or in part at the practitioners discretion. The Mass of the Holy Ghost has been replaced with the simplest form of the Latin mass, also for reasons of practicality.

As a final note, in the pages that follow we have reproduced the sigils for the demons of *The Grimorium Verum* that exist in the original. There are, however, several other demons for which no sigils are found in the *Grimorium Verum*, and, as a result are not found here. This is not an omission; they simply are not in the original.

CHAPTER THIRTEEN

The Ritual Of Lucifuge
Being The Art Of Demonic Pacts,
Based In Part Upon The Grand Grimoire
Including The Sexual Sacrifice

Preparation Of The Operator

The most favorable time for this ritual is the time of the full moon, although it may be done at other times if the magician is constrained to do so, or on special days such as Walpurgis Nacht, or All Hallows Eve.

As always the practitioner must ritually cleanse himself and abstain from intoxication and other similar diversions until the time of the major operation itself. The operator is also urged during this time to meditate on the form of the operation, and upon the articles of the pact itself, which he should now be in the process of composing.

The composition of the pact is itself a devotional act. It gives the operator the chance to consider carefully, and verbalize exactly what it is he wants from the spiritual connection he is about to make. This should be done with great care and great honesty. No other eyes need ever see this document, and when completed and signed, it will have talismanic properties, so no other person should touch it unnecessarily.

In addition to what he wants from the spirit, the operator must also consider during this time what he has that would be of service or interest to the demons. This does not particularly include the selling of one's soul, since from any point of view, damned souls are a dime a dozen.

In the pre-Christian and shamanic traditions, the demons are offered such things as: service, devotion, publicity, artistic embodiment, or participation in sexual or other acts by means of temporarily entering the magician, as in Voodoo. They are also given various kinds of offerings which can range from the traditional blood sacrifice, butchered meats, various liquors, incense or tobacco.

What the demons desire should be carefully determined by some means of divination such as the pendulum, the Tarot or the *I Ching*. What the divination says, especially if it says it repeatedly, should be taken seriously. *The operator should not deceive himself into thinking that what might be the easiest choice of offering is the one actually selected.* A disappointed demon is not a desirable companion.

The Materials & Weapons

For the operation you will need candles (red or black), a knife of new steel, a wand, a large metal dish or censer in which perfumes and other material can be burned, and most importantly, a small semi-precious stone, such as a crystal, with which to draw circles and signs on the astral. The original *Grand Grimoire* says this should be a bloodstone.

The knife should be new, or one which has long been used in ritual magic and witchcraft.

The wand should ideally be made by the operator. He should arise early, before sunrise, and go to a place where he may find trees that have grown wild. Here, just as the sun reaches the horizon, he should cut the wand from the selected tree. While doing this he should face the sun and imagine its rays passing through himself, the knife and the wand, charging them with power. When consecrated this wand will be a weapon to compel the demons to respond when called.

Among the trees traditionally used for the making of a wand are Hazel, Ash, Willow and Oak.

If the ideal situation is not possible, the wand may be made in some other more convenient way, or one that you already own may be used. The important thing is that all the instruments be ritually cleansed with water and incense before use, and that they be wrapped in clean, consecrated cloths and set aside for the evocation to follow.

During this time, no one but the magician himself should be allowed to touch any of the instruments until the evocation is finished.

It is suggested that the semi-precious stone or crystal be kept on the person of the operator during this period to "bond" with him.

THE SACRIFICE

During the time of preparation, and before the night of the evocation itself, an offering is necessary.

Historically, this was a young goat, preferably black and virgin. The magician takes the goat to the place where the evocation is to be done and, slitting its throat says:

Conjuration Of The Offering

I immolate this victim to Thee, O grand Adonay, Eloim, Ariel and Jehovam, to the honor, glory and power of Thy Name, which is superior to all spirits. O grand Adonay! Vouchsafe to receive it as an acceptable offering. Amen.

The goat or other sacrifice was then skinned and its carcass burned. The skin was cured and used as the material the pact was to be written on.

Also, an offering of meat or organs such as beef heart purchased at the supermarket may be used. However, the flesh must be either burned, as described above, or buried in or by the place of evocation.

The modern alternative that we have described as the ultimate non-animal sacrifice is a sexual sacrifice.

THE SEXUAL SUBSTITUTE

From a practical point of view ritual sex and the sexual fluids can be used in place of an animal sacrifice.

If a single person is involved in the sexual sacrifice, he or she may practice auto-eroticism and, as orgasm approaches, recite the "conjuration of the offering." He/she should then ejaculate or anoint the vaginal secretions upon the parchment prepared for the pact. Some of the secretions should be consumed by the operator allowing them to slowly dissolve in the mouth.

If a heterosexual couple is involved, the same process should apply, with one of the couple reciting the conjuration. The woman should then squat over the parchment and allow the combined sexual fluids to drip on it. Some of the fluids should be shared between the couple by oral consumption. The sharing of the fluid is also necessary if the couple is homosexual.

If the couple are homosexual and male, they should both ejaculate on the parchment.

If they are homosexual and female, both should put their vaginal fluids on the parchment.

Needless to say, the parchment must be allowed to dry thoroughly before the articles of the pact are written on it.

EVOCATION OF THE PRIME MINISTER OF HELL: LUCIFUGE

When the night selected for the pact operation arrives, and the perfected pact has been written upon the parchment, the materials and instruments should be brought to the place of evocation.

The arrangement and cleansing of the *insularium*, or place of working, is the first thing to be done.

Banishing Ritual Of The Pentagram

Facing East:

The operator should take the knife (or, if he prefers, the crystal to be used for the circle) and touching his forehead with the point, say: ATOH (ah-toh).

He then touches the heart and says: LUCIFER (or, if you are a follower of Crowley: AIWASS; or if you are Christian: IHShVH BEN JOSEPH.)

Touch the groin and say: MALKUTH (mal-kooth).

Touch the right shoulder and say: VE-GEBURAH (veh-ghee-boo-rah).

Touch the left shoulder and say: VE-GEDULAH (veh-ghee-dew-lah).

Cross the arms across the chest and say: LE-OLAM (lee-oh-lum) and vibrate: AUM.

Still facing east:

Trace a pentagram with the knife beginning with the bottom left point and tracing up to the top. Visualize the pentagram glowing white. Say: YHVH (yee-ho-vah).

With your arm outstretched turn south, trace the pentagram and say: ADONAI (a-don-eye).

In the same posture, turn west, make the pentagram and say: EHIEH (eh-hay-yeh).

Same posture, turning north say: AGLA (ah-guh-la).

Arm still outstretched, return to the east. Imagine yourself surrounded by a circle of four flaming pentagrams.

Put your arms out to your sides in the form of a cross and say:

Before me RAPHAEL, behind me GABRIEL, on my right hand MICHAEL, on my left hand URIEL. About me flames the pentagram, and in the column [visualize a column of light passing vertically through your body] stands the six-rayed star.

Finally, repeat touching the knife to forehead, heart and groin saying: ATOH, LUCIFER, MALKUTH; right shoulder: VE-GEBURAH; and left shoulder: VE-GEDULAH.

Cross the arms over the chest and say LE-OLAM, and vibrate: AUM.

Now place the censer, knife, wand and candles within the area of the circle. The circle may be drawn or made physically, but whether it is or not, it *must* be drawn astrally with the stone that has already been prepared. It may be a simple circle, or one done in one of the following forms:

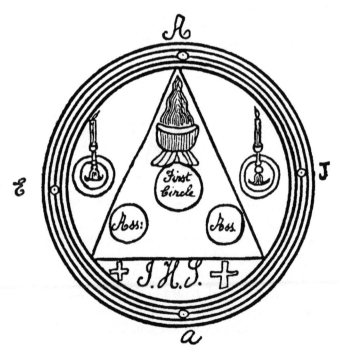

The sealing must be done only when all participants are inside.

The censer may now be lit if it has not already been. (For this operation the censer should be of the charcoal burning type since the coals are used to torment a recalcitrant demon.)

When the conjuration is recited, the operator should be *facing east*. Alertness should be maintained, however, since the spirit may manifest anywhere outside the circle, and may do so in a number of ways. There might be a change in temperature or a tingling feeling (called "vibrations" by spiritists) or even some visual manifestation (as described earlier in this book). Or one may simply experience a feeling of unease, of "being watched." It might even be suggested that a ouija board be set up in the circle if there is more than one participant. (The principle reason this excellent tool has been maligned by occult practitioners is that it works so well, and often scares them silly.)

When a manifestation occurs that makes the operator suspect the presence of the spirit, he may visualize *Lucifuge Rofocale* ("Rofocale" appears to be an anagram of the demon "Focalor" listed in several other demonologies) in his traditional form (see the illustration at the beginning of this book).

When all are in the circle, and the incense is lit, the magician says:

I present Thee, O great Adonay, this incense as the purest I can obtain; in like manner, I present Thee this charcoal prepared from the most ethereal of woods. I offer them, O grand and omnipotent Adonay, Eloim, Ariel and Jehovam, with my whole soul and my whole heart. Vouchsafe, O great Adonay, to receive them as an acceptable holocaust. Amen.

First Conjuration

(Addressed to the Emperor Lucifer):

Emperor Lucifer, Master and Prince of Rebellious Spirits, I adjure thee to leave thine abode, in whatsoever quarter of the world it may be situated, and come hither to communicate with me. I command and I conjure thee in the Name of the Mighty living God, Father, Son and Holy Ghost, to appear without noise and without any evil smell, to respond in a clear and intelligible voice, point by point, to all that I shall ask thee, failing which, thou shalt be most surely compelled to obedience by the power of the divine Adonay, Eloim, Ariel, Jehovam, Tagla, Mathon, and by the whole hierarchy of superior intelligences, who shall constrain thee against thy will. Venite, Venite! Submiritillor Lucifuge, or eternal torment shall overwhelm thee, by the great power of this blasting rod.

Second Conjuration

(If the first conjuration is ineffective):

I command and I adjure thee, Emperor Lucifer, as the representative of the mighty living God, and by the power of Emmanuel, His only Son, Who is thy master and mine, and by the virtue of His precious blood, which He shed to redeem mankind from thy chains, I command thee to quit thine abode, wheresoever it may be, swearing that I will give thee one quarter of an hour alone, if thou dost not straightway come hither and communicate with me in an audible and intelligible voice, or, if thy personal presence be impossible, dispatch me thy Messenger Astaroth in a human form, without either noise or evil smell, failing which I will smite thee and thy whole race with the terrible Blasting Rod into the depth of the bottomless abysses, and that by the power of those great words in the Clavicle—by Adonay, Eloim, Ariel, Jehovam, Tagla, Mathon, Almouzin,

Arios, Pithona, Magots, Sylphae, Tabots, Salamandrae, Gnomus, Terrae, Coelis, Godens, Aqua.

If, after this, the spirit does not respond, plunge your wand into the brazier or censer to torment him, and visualize this occurring. Then recite:

Third Conjuration

I adjure thee, Emperor Lucifer, as the agent of the strong living God, of His beloved Son and of the Holy Ghost, and by the power of the Great Adonay, Eloim, Ariel and Jehovam, to appear instantly, or to send thy Messenger Astaroth, forcing thee to forsake thy hiding-place, wheresoever it may be, and warning thee that if thou dost not manifest this moment, I will straightway smite thee and all thy race with the Blasting Rod of the great Adonay, Eloim, Ariel and Jehovam.

If the spirit should still not cooperate, plunge the wand once again into the fire and say:

Grand Conjuration

I adjure thee, O Spirit! by the power of the grand Adonay, to appear instanter, and by Eloim, by Ariel, by Jehovam, by Aqua, Tagla, Mathon, Oarios, Almozin, Arios, Membrot, Varios, Pithona, Majods, Sulphae, Gabots, Salamandrae, Tabots, Gingua, Janna, Etitnamus, Zariatnatmix, A. E. A. J. A. T. M. O. A. A. M. V. P. M. S. C. S. J. C. G. A. J. F. Z.
[These initials represent the various names of God such as Adonay, Tetragrammaton, Metatron, etc.]

The operator is enjoined to be patient during the evocation, until results occur. At this point, he must consult with the demon and negotiate agreement to the pact in whatever mode of communication he has selected (ouija board, pendulum, clairvoyance, and so forth).

Or, the practitioner may use:

Grand Conjuration Of Spirits
With Whom It Is Sought To Make A Pact

Emperor Lucifer, Master of all the revolted Spirits, I entreat thee to favor me in the adjuration which I address to thee mighty minister, Lucifuge Rofocale, being desirous to make a pact with him. I beg thee also, O Prince Beelzebuth, to protect me in my undertaking. O Count Astaroth! Be propitious to me, and grant that tonight the great Lucifuge may appear to me under a human form, free from evil smell, and that he may accord me, in virtue of the pact which I propose to enter into, all the riches that I need. O grand Lucifuge, I pray thee to quit thy dwelling, wheresoever it may be, and come hither to speak with me; otherwise will I compel thee by the power of the strong living God, His beloved Son and the Holy Spirit. Obey the potent words in the grand Clavicle of Solomon, wherewith he was accustomed to compel the rebellious spirits to receive his compact. Then straightway appear, or I will persistently torture thee by the virtue of these great words in the Clavicle: Aglon, Tetragram, Vaycheon Stimulamaton Ezphares Retragrammaton Olyaram Irion Esytion Existion Eryona Onera Orasym Mozm Messias Soter Emmanuel Sabaoth Adonay, te adoro, te invoco. Amen

The adept may choose to use the above conjuration in place of all others.

When the pact has been executed the closing:

Conjuration & Discharge Of The Spirit

O Prince Lucifer, I am, for the time, contented with thee. I now leave thee in peace, and permit thee to retire wheresoever it may seem good to thee, so it be without noise and without leaving any evil smell behind thee. Be mindful, however, of our engagement, for shouldst thou fail in it, even for a moment, be assured that I shall eternally smite thee with the Blasting Rod of the great Adonay, Eloim, Ariel and Jehovam. Amen.

The magician now closes with the banishing pentagram ritual described earlier.

He now retires, or if he chooses, enjoys a feast.

CHAPTER FOURTEEN

The Grimorium Verum

PUBLISHED BY ALIBECK THE EGYPTIAN,
AT MEMPHIS, 1517

Translated from the Hebrew by Plaingeire, *Jesuit Dominicaine,* with a collection of Curious Secrets. The True Clavicles of Solomon.

INTRODUCTION

The first part of what follows contains various symbols, by which powers the devils are invoked. This allows the operator to make them appear when he desires each according to their rank and their power, and to deliver what the operator has asked.

This can be done without difficulties *as long as the devils have been appeased.* It is imperative to keep in mind that these forces give nothing for nothing: *they demand payment.*

Also the operator should note that there is a method of calling forth the elementals: that is, the forces or inhabitants of Earth, Air, Sea, or *Infernus* according to their specific nature.

The second part of the book teaches secrets of both natural and supernatural forces that have been empowered by the demons. Using these methods properly will help the operator from being grossly deceived or manipulated.

In the third section the operator will find the clavicle or key to the workings, and the way of employing them.

THE FIRST PART

There are three great Infernal Powers, the triune are: *Lucifer, Beelzebuth* and *Astaroth*. Their symbols must be engraved in the correct manner and at the appropriate hours. Everything must be done exactly.

Males must carry the symbol with them in their right pocket. The symbol must be written with your own blood or the blood of a sea-turtle.

Place within the circle of the sigil the first letters of your first and last name. If you desire greater power, draw the symbol of the personage on an emerald or ruby, as they have a great affinity with the spirits, particularly those of the Sun, who are of greater virtue than the others.

Always create the symbol on the day and in the hour of Mars.

Females should carry the symbol of the personage on their left side, between the breasts, like a Reliquary.

Be sure to follow the instructions exactly if you wish the spirits to obey you.

The exalted spirits of great rank and power serve only their confidantes and intimate friends, by the *pact* made according to certain symbols at the instruction of *Singambuth* or of his Secretary. *Aabidandes* (sometimes thought to be Singambuth's secretary) is an ideal personage to call, conjure and constrain for this purpose. The details for this will be dilated upon later.

THE TWO KINDS OF PACTS

There are only two kinds of pacts which may be made with the demons: the tacit and the explicit. When you make a pact with a spirit, and must pay with something that belongs to you, but you must be on your guard that he does not exact from you more than he deserves or than you are willing to give. Nonetheless, fair payment must be made, and with something the demon desires.

THE VARIETIES OF SPIRITS

There are superior and inferior spirits. The superior spirits are: *Lucifer, Beelzebuth* and *Astaroth*. The inferiors of *Lucifer* reside in Europe and Asia. These will be listed later. *Beelzebuth* lives in Africa and *Astaroth* makes his home in America.

Lucifer, Beelzebuth and *Astaroth* each have two chief officers who inform the lesser demons of what Emperor *Lucifer* has decided to do in the world. They also report to Lucifer the results of his decisions and other activities.

THE MANNER IN WHICH
THE SPIRITS APPEAR WHEN CALLED

Being of pure Mind and not made of "matter" the spirits do not necessarily appear in the same shape at all times. They find or create a body for themselves which will suit their purposes.

Lucifer manifests himself as a beautiful boy. When he is angry he is red in color.

Beelzebuth appears, when he desires (which is frequently) in grotesque and distorted forms. He favors the forms of a giant cow, or a great ram with a long tail. He vomits fire when enraged.

Astaroth appears as human, but with skin as black as ink.

Below are *Lucifer's* circle and his symbols:

And the circles and symbols of *Beelzebuth* and *Astaroth*:

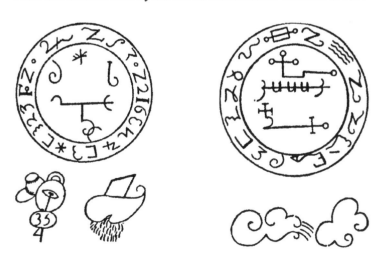

To Call The Spirits

When you desire to call upon the spirits, you simply write their symbols on parchment or some other medium which the demons have given as a gift to mankind for their use.

The Inferior Spirits

The inferior spirits below *Lucifer* are *Satanachia* and *Agalierap*.

The inferior spirits below *Beelzebuth* are *Tarchmache* and *Fleruty*.

The symbols of *Satanachia* and *Fleruty* are:

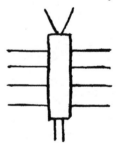 

The inferior spirits to *Astaroth* are *Sagatana* and *Nesbiros*. Their symbols are:

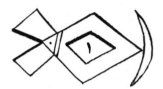 

THE SECOND PART
AGLA * ADONAY * JEHOVAH

There are other demons, besides those listed above, which are under the power of Duke *Syrach*, and must be called in his name.

They are:

Clauneck has power over goods, money and finances; he can discover hidden treasures to him who makes pact with him; he can bestow great wealth, for he is well loved by *Lucifer*. He brings money from a distance. Obey him and he will obey thee.

Musisin has power over great lords; he instructs them in all that passes in the Republics and the realms of the Allies.

Bechard has power over winds and tempests, over lightning, hail and rain, by means of a charm with toads and other things of this nature.

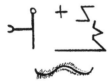

Frimost has power over wives and maids and will help thee to enjoy them.

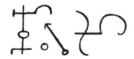

Klepoth brings dreams and visions of all kinds.

Khil occasions great earthquakes.

Mersilde can transport thee instantaneously wheresoever may be desired.

Clistheret makes day or night about thee at pleasure.

Sirchade has power to show thee all kinds of animals, of whatsoever nature they may be.

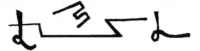

Segal causes all manner of prodigies visibly, both natural and supernatural.

Hiepacth will bring thee a distant person in an instant.

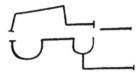

Humots can transport all manner of books for thy pleasure.

Frucissiere brings the dead to life.

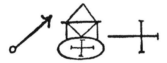

Guland can cause all varieties of disease.

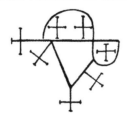

Surgat opens all locks.

Morail has the power to make everything in the world invisible.

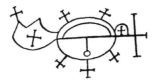

Frutimiere dights thee all kinds of festivals.

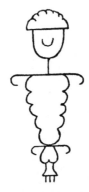

Huicthgara occasions sleep and waking in some, and afflicts others with insomnia.

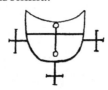

Satanachia and *Satanaciae* govern fifty-four demons, four of whom are *Serguthy, Heramael, Trimasel* and *Sustugriel.* These four—who are the only ones of importance to the magician—will aid him well, if they are pleased with him. (To come to terms with these, you must call upon them in the name of their superiors—*Satanachia* and *Satanaciae*—and demand to be given their symbols as signature for the pact.)

Serguthy has power over wives and virgins, when the occasion is favorable.

Heramael teaches the art of medicine, gives absolute knowledge of all diseases, with their full and radical cure, makes known all plants in general, the places where they grow, the times of their gathering, their virtues also and their composition for the attainment of a perfect cure.

Trimasel teaches chemistry and all sleight of hand. He imparts the true secret for confecting the powder of projection which changes imperfect metals—lead, iron, pewter, copper and quicksilver—into true good silver and good gold, namely, Sun and Moon, according to the ferment thereof. Only he must be satisfied with the operator, if the operator would be satisfied with him.

Sustugriel teaches magical art; he gives familiar spirits for all things that can be desired; and furnishes mandragores.

Agalierept and *Tarihimal* govern *Elelogap*, who has power over the element of water.

Nebirots rules *Hael* and *Sergulath*. *Hael* instructs in the art of writing all kinds of letters, gives an immediate power of speaking all kinds of tongues and explains the most secret things. *Sergulath* furnishes every manner of speculation, teaches tactics and the breaking of hostile ranks.

These are their inferiors, who have great power:

Proculo, who gives sleep for twenty-four hours, with knowledge of the spheres of sleep.

Haristum, who gives the power of passing unsinged through the fire.

Brulefer, who makes one loved.

Pentagnony, who renders one invisible and also beloved by great lords.

Aglasis, who transports through the whole world.

Sidragrosam, who makes girls dance stark naked.

Minoson, who insures winning in all games.

Bucon, who has the power to excite hatred and jealousy between the sexes.

THE THIRD PART

The Invocation

[The crosses in the text below, and elsewhere, signify that the magician should make the sign of a cross with his hand, wand or knife where indicated.]

HELOY ✠ TAU ✠ VARAF ✠ PANTHON ✠
HOMNORCUM ✠ ELEMIATH ✠ SERUGEATH ✠
AGLA ✠ ON ✠ TETRAGRAMMATON ✠ CASILY

This is to be written on unused (virgin) parchment paper with the symbol of the demon (or his name, in absence of a symbol), which will cause the messenger *Scirlin* to come. Beneath him are all the others, and the appearance of the others requires speech with him first. He is one of the messengers of Hell and can force the other demons to appear for the operator whether they will or no, as he represents the authority of *Lucifer*.

Preparation Of The Operator

(Done during the bath of the Art when the Sorcerer purifies himself in readiness.)

Recite the following Orison:

Lord God Adonay, who hast crated man from earth to reflect Thine own image and likeness, who has created me also, unworthy as I am, deign, I pray Thee, ✠ to bless this water, that it may be healthful to my body and soul, that all delusion and ill will may depart from me. *O Lord God, Almighty and Ineffable, Who didst lead forth Thy people from the land of Egypt, and didst cause them to pass dry-shod over the Red Sea! Grant that I may be cleansed by this water from all my impieties and may appear blameless before Thee. Amen*

When the operator has been thus purified, he must begin the manufacture of the Instruments of the Art.

The Knife

Make or purchase a new knife at the day and hour of Jupiter. Now, charge the knife with the following conjuration on the day and in the hour of Venus:

I conjure thee, O form of this instrument, by the authority of God the Father Almighty, by the virtue of Heaven and the stars, of the Angels, of the elements, of stones and herbs, by the power of the forces of nature.

I beg that this all be accepted in the perfection in which it is offered, without trickery, falsehood or deception, by the command of God, Creator of the ages and Emperor of the Angels. Amen.

Now say: *Damahii, Lumech, Gadal, Pancia, Veloas, Meorod, Lamidoch, Baldach, Anerethon, Mitatron, most holy angels, be ye wardens of this instrument, because I shall make use of it for several necessary works.*

Place the knife in a new wrapper of red silk, making suffumigations with perfumes as will hereinafter be set forth.

The Sacrificial Knife

On the day of Mars, at the new moon, make (or buy) another knife of new steel, mark or engrave on the handle this sign:

$$\mathcal{G} 2 \mathcal{J} \mathcal{J}$$

Then write or engrave the name AGLA upon the blade.
Asperge and fumigate it. The instrument is now ready for
use as you desire.

THE METHOD OF ASPERGING & FUMIGATION

The Asperser

An asperser is made by binding bunches of mint, marjo-
ram and rosemary with a thread which has been made by a
virgin maiden. It is to be done in the day and hour of Mercury, during the new moon. This is then dipped in exorcised water (described below) and used to asperge and
purify whatever is needed.

The Perfumes

The perfumes for the fumigations are to be aloes, wood,
incense and mace. For the fumigation of the magic circle,
mace alone is to be used. Before use, the operators supply
of perfumes should be blessed thus:

Orison of the Aromatic Perfumes:
*O creature of perfume, be sanctified by the Lord, that you
may be a remedy for our souls and bodies through his holy
Name! Agree that all creatures that may breathe your
vapors will have wealth of body and soul: Through the
Lord that has fashioned eternal time! Amen.*

The Aspersion Of The Water

The water used in all these operations must be asperged
and exorcised by saying over it:

Adonay, I entreat thee to bless this water, in the hope that it may purify our bodies and souls through Thee most holy Adonay, Ruler Everlasting. Amen.

The orison, to be recited during the asperging:

In the name of the Ineffable and Immortal God, I Asperge (Name of the instrument), and cleanse you of all untrust-worthiness and untruth and you shall be pure as the new fallen snow. Amen.

Pour the blessed water used in the asperging after this, saying:

In the name of the Father, and of the Son and of the Holy Spirit, Amen.

Asperge and fumigate every item used in the ritual.

To fumigate the instruments, burn incense and pass the instrument through it saying:

Angels of God, come to my aid, and enable my work to be accomplished. Zalay, Salmay, Dalmay, Angrecton, Ledrion, Amisor, Euchey, Or. Great Angels: Come to me also O, Adonay, come and give this life and virtue so that this creature (meaning the instrument) may have form and by this my work accomplished. In the Name of the Father, and of the Son, and of the Holy Spirit. Amen.

THE VIRGIN PARCHMENT

Historically, virgin parchment was made from the skin of a goat, lamb, or calf, or some other animal, which has never mated. The pact was often written on this, made from the sacrificed animal. In our modern society, this is often not practical. Therefore, sprinkling some blood or other fluid on a piece of expensive paper will suffice.

When the sacrifice is made to begin the process of making the parchment, all of the instruments must already have been made and placed upon the altar.

THE ROD OF THE ART

The rod must be made from virgin hazel wood. It must be cut with the knife of the art with a single quick stroke. This is done on the day and the hour of Mercury when the moon is new. Engrave it with the pen or lancet using the seal and sigil of *Frimost*.

Make another rod of virgin hazel wood. Cut it on the day and hour of the Sun, and engrave upon it the seal and sigil of Klippoth.

Now say this Orison over the rods:

Oh! Adonay, most Holy and most Powerful, vouchsafe to consecrate and bless this rod so that it may possess the required virtue, Oh most Holy Adonay, to whom be Glory for ever and ever. Amen.

THE LANCET

A lancet must be made or purchased in the manner of the knives. This must be done on the day and in the hour of Mercury at the new moon. It must be asperged and fumigated in the manner described above.

THE PEN OF THE ART

Take a new quill and asperge and fumigate it in the same fashion as the other instruments. While doing this say:

Ababaloy, Samoy, Escavor, Adonay: From this quill remove all deviousness so that it may hold the power of truth. Amen.

THE INK-HORN

Purchase an new ink-horn or bottle on the day and in the hour of Mercury. It should be an unmarked ink-horn (or bottle) as the God names below must be written upon it:

JOD HE VAU HE METATRON JOD KADOS ELYM SABAOTH

Before the ink is used, it must be exorcised thus:

I exorcise thee, creature of Ink, by Anston, Cerreton, Stimulator, Adonay, and by the name of Him Whose one Word created all and can achieve all, that so thou shalt assist me in my work, that my work may be accomplished by my will, and fulfilled with the permission of God, Who ruleth in all things and through all things, everywhere and forever. Amen.

THE SACRIFICE

(Note: What follows is for historical reference only.)

Take your goat (or other animal)—place it on an altar. Take the sacrificial knife and cut the throat with a single stroke while pronouncing the name of the demon that you wish to call up:

"I kill you in the name and to the honor of N…"

The throat must be severed with a single stroke.

Skin the animal with the knife (distinct from the sacrificial knife; bear in mind which one you are to use), and while doing so, say this:

Invocation

Adonay, Dalmay, Lauday, Tetragrammaton, Anereton, and all Holy Angels of God, come to me and infuse into the hide the power that preserves it as well as all that is written upon it may become as perfect as God.

After skinning the animal and stretching the skin, take salt and spread this upon the skin, covering it well. Before the salt is put upon the skin, the following benediction must be said:

Benediction Of The Salt

I exorcise you, O creature of salt by the living God, that all deceit may leave you and you may be worthy of our holy parchment.

Place the salted skin in the sun for one full day.

Write these characters around it with the pen of the art:

(At this point there followed a series of complicated and now unnecessary processes for curing the skin. As said earlier, the blood of the sacrifice placed on the fine parchment will suffice. If you do wish to use the skin, simply clean it and dry it.)

The skin is allowed to dry, but before leaving it, say over it:

Je, Agla, Jod, Hoi, He, Emmanuel! Protect and guard this parchment, so that no evil influence may take hold of it!

The operator must abstain from intercourse (unless it is ritual intercourse as defined elsewhere in this text) during the manufacture of this parchment. [This is one of several remarkable pagan survivals in these rituals—The editors.]

THE PREPARATION OF THE OPERATOR

When the Instruments of the Art have been made, the operator must get himself ready.

First, the Preparatory Orison must be recited at the ritual bath:

Adonay, in whose image I am formed, I beseech Thee to bless this water for the benefit of my soul, and cleanse me of my imperfections.

In addition to the ritual bath before working, the operator must remain chaste and free from mortal sin for three days before the beginning of major work, before calling up one of the fallen, and while making the Virgin Parchment.

(Except of course if a ritual sexual operation is being performed. It is important to keep in mind that no sex outside of the ritual sex act should be performed.)

During the time of purification, the operator should study and meditate upon this book, and pray five times during the day and four times during the night, with the following prayer:

Astrochio, Asath, a sacra Bedrimubal, Felut, Anabotos, Serablilem, Sergen, Gemen, Domos: O my God, who art enthroned higher than the Heavens, Thou who seeth even in the heart of all things, I pray that Thou fulfill my desires and grant me success. Amen.

On the day and hour of Mars, (the first hour on Tuesday, just before sunrise) inscribe on a piece of virgin parchment with all the characters of the spirits that you wish to call up. Drawing blood from a finger or your arm, use it to draw the insignia of *Scirlin*, which is necessary to compel the demons to come.

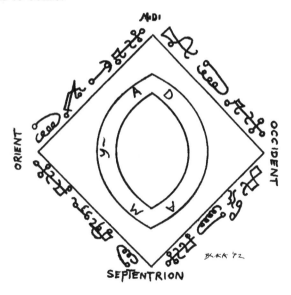

The Seal Of Scirlin

Invocation To Scirlin

Helon, Taul, Varf, Pan, Heon, Homonoreum, Clemialh, Serugeath, Agla, Tetragrammaton, Casoly.

Write the first letter of your name next to the letter 'A' on the sigil (see the character of Scirlin above) and the first letter of your last name next to the letter 'D' on the sigil. This part of the sigil is associated with the demon *Aglassis*, a potent spirit who will give you power over lesser demons.

The character of *Scirlin* must be made upon the parchment, above the characters of the other demons that you desire to conjure. After which make the appropriate conjurations below, and burn incense in their honor.

OF THE CIRCLE OF EVOCATION

When you lay your circle, before entering and sealing it, it must be perfumed with musk, amber, aloes wood and incense.

Also, you must always have a fire, or brazier with coals burning within the circle, for suffumigations, and when you place the perfume upon the fire, repeat:

I offer this perfume in the name and to the honor of N...

You must hold the invocation or book in your left hand and the wand in your right. The knife should be at your feet.

Construct the circle with the knife of the art and draw a pentacle at each of the cardinal points of the compass outside it. During the consecration of the circle, the spirit or spirits to be called are specifically prohibited from entering the circle.

When you are in the circle, you must repeat the appropriate invocations seven times (the sacred number of the planets) and when the spirit appears, cause him to sign or acknowledge your possession of his sigil on the parchment that you hold, and swear obedience. Make him promise to come whenever you call upon him, without hesitation or resistance. Ask for what you desire and need and he will give it to you.

CONJURATION FOR LUCIFER

Lucifer, Ouyar, Chameron, Aliseon, Mandousin, Premy, Oriet, Naydru, Esmony, Eparinesont, Estiot, Dumosson, Danochar, Casmiel, Hayras, Fabelleronthou, Sodirno, Peatham, Venite, Venite, LUCIFER. Amen

CONJURATION FOR BEELZEBUTH

Beelzebuth, Lucifer, Madilon, Solymo, Saroy, Theu, Ameclo, Segrael, Praredun, Adricanorom, Martino, Timo, Cameron, Phorsy, Metosite, Prumosy, Dumaso, Elvisa, Alphrois, Fubentroty, Venite, Venite, BEELZEBUTH. Amen.

CONJURATION FOR ASTAROTH

Astaroth, Ador, Cameso, Valuerituf, Mareso, Lodir, Cadomir, Aluiel, Calniso, Tely, Plorim, Viordy, Cureviorbas, Cameron, Vesturiel, Vulnavij, Benez meus Calmiron, Noard, Nisa Chenibranbo Calevodium, Brazo Tabrasol, Venite, Venite, ASTAROTH. Amen.

For how to deal with the manifestations of demons, you are referred to comments made in the Ritual of Lucifuge and to the personal experiences of Jason Black.

DISMISSAL OF THE SPIRITS

After performing the above operation and being satisfied that the spirits were present, you may dismiss them with the following:

Ite in pace ad loca vestra et pax sit inter vos redituri ad mecum vos invocavero, in nomine Patris ✠ et Filii ✠ et Spiritus Sancti ✠ Amen.

Conjuration For Lesser Spirits

After each name of power the magician should make a cross in the air with the wand or knife:

Osurny ✠ *delumsan* ✠ *atalsloym* ✠ *charusihoa* ✠ *melany liamintho* ✠ *colehon* ✠ *paron* ✠ *madoin* ✠ *merloy* ✠ *bulerator donmedo* ✠ *lone* ✠ *peloym* ✠ *ibasil* ✠ *meon* ✠ *alymdrictels* ✠ *person crisolsay* ✠ *lemon sessle nidar horiel peunt* ✠ *halmon* ✠ *asophiel* ✠ *ilnostreon* ✠ *baniel* ✠ *vermias* ✠ *slevor* ✠ *noelma* ✠ *dorsamot* ✠ *lhavala* ✠ *omor* ✠ *frangam* ✠ *beldor* ✠ *dragin* ✠ *Venite, Venite,* N...

Dismissal Of Lesser Spirits

Use the dismissal in Latin above.

The Pentacles Of Solomon, Son Of David

Here is put the form of the Pentacle of Solomon, for defense against rebellious spirits:

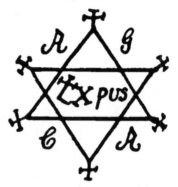

(This is also Agrippa's seal.)

The Construction Of The Mirror Of Solomon

The Mirror of Solomon is useful in divination and in speaking with the spirits. When properly made and consecrated, you may see in this mirror anything that you may desire.

Remain chaste and pure when you begin this operation. Avoid anger and strong emotion. Take a plate of steel, polished to a mirror finish, slightly curved. Sacrifice a white pigeon to bring life to the mirror, and with its blood write at the four corners these names: JEHOVAH, ELOYM, METATRON, ADONAY. Wrap the steel in a clean white cloth. Look for the new Moon, just after the sun has gone below the horizon, and address it thus:

O Eternal, O Lord Eternal! Thou who hast created all things deign to look upon me, N..., thy most unworthy servant and upon this, which is my will.

Send the angel Anael into this mirror. He who leads and controls his peers that he and they may show and do all that I desire.

Throw upon the brazier that you have burning, perfume of saffron, which is proper to this operation. While burning the perfume you say three times:

In your name I do this oh God Triune exalted judge who sits above the Archangels hear me.

When you have done this, breathe three times upon the mirror's surface and say:

CONJURATION FOR ANAEL

Come, Anael, come: Be with me willingly in the name of the most high and of the Son and of the Holy Spirit.

Come Anael, in the name of Jehovah, Metatron and Elohim.

Come to me, Anael [said over the mirror] *and order thy subjects to make known to me that which lies hidden from my eyes.*

Now make the sign of the cross upon yourself and over the mirror. Place the mirror where you can see into it clearly, and without obstruction. Set a burning candle on either side of it.

The angel Anael will appear as a beautiful child. He will greet you and cause his siblings and servants to obey you. Ask of him what you desire and he will show it to you within the mirror.

When you wish to see Anael again, set up the mirror and recite the conjuration given above. When not in use, the mirror must be kept wrapped in its cloth and hidden away.

The Dismissal Of Anael

When he or his siblings have answered your questions to your satisfaction, you send them away by saying:

I thank thee Anael, for having appeared and having fulfilled my requests. Thou mayest therefore go in peace, and shall return when I command thee.

Divination By The Word Of Anael

[This operation was performed by Count Cagliostro, early in his magical career in France—The editors.]

Locate a place that for nine days or more has not been visited by women who are menstruating.

The room must be cleansed by consecrations, aspersions and suffumigations. In the center of the room place a table covered with a white cloth. On the table place a new glass bottle or vial filled with pure spring water, and three small tapers made of virgin wax mixed with human fat; add a piece of virgin parchment, the quill of a bird made into a pen, fresh ink and a brazier ready to be lit.

To aid in this operation, you should have a small boy, of nine or ten, who is clean and well behaved. He sits near the table.

The tapers should be positioned to the right, left and behind a vial of water. Light the brazier and the tapers saying:

Gabamiah, Adonay, Agla, Lord of hosts be with us!

At the right of the glass place the parchment; the pen and ink should be on the left. Tell the boy to look deeply into the vial and speaking gently into his right ear, say:

The Conjuration

Uriel, Seraph, Josata, Ablati, Agla, Caila, I conjure thee by the four words that God spoke with His mouth to Moses: Josta, Agla, Caila, Ablati—and by the Nine Heavens—also by the virginity of this child to appear, at once, and visibly to disclose precisely that information which I desire to know. And when this is done, I shall discharge thee in benevolence, in the Name of Adonay.

When this has been done, ask the boy whether he sees an image in the vial. If he sees an angel or other form in the glass, the magician shall address it in a amicable manner:

Divine Spirit, I welcome thee. I bring thee forth again, in the Name of Adonay, to reveal to me forthwith [here ask your question.]

If thou dost not desire what thou sayest to be perceived by others, I demand thee to write the answer upon this parchment between now and tomorrow. Otherwise disclose the answer to my request in my sleep.

If the spirit answers, listen courteously. If he does not speak, after the entreaty has been repeated three times, extinguish the tapers and leave the chamber until the next day. Return in the morning and you will find the answer written on the parchment, or it will have been given you in the night.

DIVINATION BY THE EGG

[It was this operation, taught by an island woman named Tituba to the young girls of Salem, that started the Salem witch panic at the end of the seventeenth century—The editors.]

The operation of the egg is designed to know the future.

Take the egg of a black hen, break it, and remove the germ.

Have ready a large glass, very clear, filled with pure water. Pour the egg germ into the glass.

The glass is placed so the sun shines through it at noon on a summer day.

The Master of the operation recites such conjurations as he thinks to be appropriate for the purpose, and with his index finger, stirs the water to make the germ turn. Let the water slowly come to a stop, and, not touching it, look through the glass. There you will see the answer to your question revealed in the form that the egg-germ takes. The operator must read intuitively the form that the egg takes in the water once it is still.

Operation To Make A Lover Come To You, However Modest Or Reluctant

[This operation also seems to be an old folk-magic survival from pagan times—The editors.]

Take a piece of virgin parchment, and write on it the name of the person whom you wish to compel. Below is the character to be marked upon the parchment around the name:

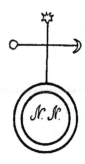

Upon the reverse side, inscribe the words *Melchidael, Bareschas*. Then place the parchment on the ground with the person's name face downward. Put your right foot on the parchment, and your left knee, bent, on the ground. This should be done outside, at night, or in some place where the nighttime sky can be seen. Look for the risen moon, and a star, and hold them both in your vision. In your right hand, hold a lit taper of white wax. Then say:

Conjuration

I hail and conjure thee, O radiant Moon, O most exquisite Star, O brilliant light which I have in my hand. By the forces of my body I command thee. By all the names of the spirit princes living in you. By the Name ON, which created everything! By you O radiant Angel Gabriel, with the Prince of the Planet Mercury, Michael and Melchidael.

I adjure you once again, by Tetragrammaton, that you may deliver a force to torment N..., so she/he whose name is written here, shall submit to my desires forsaking all others for so long as she/he shall remain enchanted by me.

Go! Go Melchidael, Baresches, Zazel, Firiel, Malcha, and all your companions. I conjure you by Adonay to obey me and I swear to satisfy you.

When this has been said three times, singe the parchment with the taper. On the next morning, take the parchment and place it in your left shoe and leave it until the person whom you have called seeks you out. In the conjuration, you must specify the date that she/he is to come.

CHAPTER FIFTEEN

The Constitution Of
Pope Honorius The Great

The reader familiar with Waite and certain other sources should note that some small deletions have been made in the ritual to make it even remotely doable. Even with the changes we have made in this long and complex ritual, the practitioner will want to use his own judgment in timing, among other things. It is also suggested that the practitioner read through the ritual carefully and make a list of the materials needed, which are many and varied.

INTRODUCTION TO THE GRIMOIRE OF HONORIUS

"The Holy Apostolic Chair, unto which the keys of the Kingdom of Heaven were given by those words that Christ Jesus addressed to St. Peter: I give unto thee the Keys of the Kingdom of Heaven, and unto thee alone the power of commanding the Prince of Darkness and his angels, who, as slaves of their Master, do owe him honor, glory and obedience, by those other words of Christ Jesus: Thou shalt worship the Lord thy God, and Him only shalt thou serve— hence by the power of these Keys the Head of the Church has been made the Lord of Hell. But seeing that until this present the Sovereign Pontiffs have alone possessed the power of using invocations and commanding Spirits, His holiness Honorius the Third, being moved by his pastoral care, has benignly desired to communicate the methods and faculty of invoking and controlling Spirits to his venerable Brethren in Jesus Christ, adding the Conjurations which must be used in such case, the whole being contained in the Bull which here follows."

THE BULL OF POPE HONORIUS III

"Servant of the Servants of God, unto all and each of our venerable Brethren of the Holy Roman Church, Cardinals, Archbishops, Bishops, Abbots; unto all and each of our sons in Jesus Christ, Priests, Deacons, Subdeacons, Acolytes, Exorcists, Cantors, Pastors, Clerks both Secular and Regular, Health and Apostolic Benediction. In those days when the Son of God, Savior of the World, generated in the fullness of time, and born, according to the flesh, of the Race of David, did live on this earth, Whose Most Holy Name is Jesus, before which the heavens, earth and hell do bend the knee; we have seen with what power He commanded demons, which power was also transmitted to St. Peter by that utterance: Upon this rock I will build my Church, and the Gates of Hell shall not prevail against it. These words were addressed to St. Peter as the head and Foundation of the Church. We then, who, by the mercy of God, and despite the poverty of our merit, have succeeded to the Sovereign Apostolate, and, as lawful successor of St. Peter, have the Keys of the Kingdom of Heaven committed to our hands, desiring to communicate the power of invoking and commanding Spirits, which hath been reserved unto us alone, and our possessors did alone enjoy; wishing, I repeat, by Divine inspiration, to share it with our venerable Brethren and dear sons in Jesus Christ, and fearing lest in the exorcism of the possessed, they might otherwise be appalled at the frightful figures of those rebellious angels who in sin were cast into the abyss, lest also they should be insufficiently learned in those things which must be performed and observed, and that those who have been redeemed by the blood of Jesus Christ may not be tormented by witchcraft or possessed by the demon, we have included in the Bull the manner of their invocation, which same must be observed inviolably. And because it is meet that the ministers of the Altar should have authority over the rebellious Spirits, we hereby depute unto them all powers which we possess, in virtue of the Holy Apostolic Chair, and we require them, by our Apostolic authority, to observe what follows inviolably, lest by some negligence unworthy of their character they should draw down on themselves the wrath of the Most High."

Preparation

The magician, first, must fast for three days in order to purify himself for the coming task. After the three days have passed, he is to go to confession and approach the altar of the church. On the following day, he is to arise early in the morning, bathe himself, and recite the following on his knees:

[In the original the "priest" was to recite the seven gradual psalms. We have replaced this Catholic exercise with the following psalms, which were selected for their power and meanings. The operator may use all of them, or select the one most fitting his mood and motives. —The Editors.]

Psalm 29:

Give unto the Lord, O ye mighty, give unto the Lord glory and strength.

Give unto the Lord the glory due unto his name; worship the Lord in the beauty of holiness.

The voice of the Lord is upon the waters: the God of glory thundereth: the Lord is upon many waters.

The voice of the Lord is powerful; the voice of the Lord is full of majesty.

The voice of the Lord breaketh the cedars; yea, the Lord breaketh the cedars of Lebanon.

He maketh them also to skip like a calf; Lebanon and Sirion like a young unicorn.

The voice of the Lord divideth the flames of fire.

The voice of the Lord shaketh the wilderness; the Lord shaketh the wilderness of Kadesh.

The voice of the Lord maketh the hinds to calve, and discovereth the forests: and in his temple doth every one speak of his glory.

The Lord sitteth upon the flood; yea, the Lord sitteth King forever.

The Lord will give strength unto his people; the Lord will bless his people with peace.

Psalm 1:

Blessed is the man that walketh not in the counsel of the ungodly, nor standeth in the way of sinners, nor sitteth in the seat of the scornful.

But his delight is in the law of the Lord; and in his law doth he meditate day and night.

And he shall be like a tree planted by the rivers of water, that bringeth forth his fruit in his season; his leaf also shall not wither; and whatsoever he doeth shall prosper.

The ungodly are no so: but are like the chaff which the wind driveth away.

Therefore the ungodly shall not stand in the judgment, nor sinners in the congregation of the righteous.

For the Lord knoweth the way of the righteous: but the way of the ungodly shall perish.

Psalm 3:

Lord, how are they increased that trouble me! Many are they that rise up against me.

Many there be which say of my soul, There is no help for him in God. Selah.

But thou, O Lord, art a shield for me; my glory, and the lifter up of mine head.

I cried unto the Lord with my voice, and he heard me out of his holy hill. Selah.

I laid me down and slept; I awaked; for the Lord sustained me.

I will not be afraid of ten thousands of people, that have set themselves against me round about.

Arise, O Lord; save me, O my God: for thou hast smitten all mine enemies upon the cheek bone; thou hast broken the teeth of the ungodly.

Salvation belongeth unto the Lord: thy blessing is upon thy people. Selah.

Psalm 13:

How long wilt thou forget me, O Lord? for ever? how long wilt thou hide thy face from me?

How long shall I take counsel in my soul, having sorrow in my heart daily? how long shall mine enemy be exalted over me?

Consider and hear me, O Lord my God: lighten mine eyes, lest I sleep the sleep of death;

Lest mine enemy say, I have prevailed against him; and those that trouble me rejoice when I am moved.

But I have trusted in thy mercy; my heart shall rejoice in thy salvation.

I will sing unto the Lord, because he hath dealt bountifully with me.

Psalm 18:

I will love thee, O Lord, my strength.

The Lord is my rock, and my fortress, and my deliverer; my God, my strength, in whom I will trust; my buckler, and the horn of my salvation, and my high tower.

I will call upon the Lord, who is worthy to be praised: so shall I be saved from mine enemies.

The sorrows of death compassed me, and the floods of ungodly men made me afraid.

The sorrows of Hell compassed me about: the snares of death prevented me.

In my distress I called upon the Lord, and cried unto my God: he heard my voice out of his temple, and my cry came before him, even into his ears.

Then the earth shook and trembled; the foundations also of the hills moved and were shaken, because he was wroth.

There went up a smoke out of his nostrils, and fire out of his mouth devoured: coals were kindled by it.

He bowed the heavens also, and came down: and darkness was under his feet.

And he rode upon a cherub, and did fly: yea, he did fly upon the wings of the wind.

He made darkness his secret place; his pavilion round about him were dark waters and thick clouds of the skies.

At the brightness that was before him his thick clouds passed, hail stones and coals of fire.

The Lord also thundered in the heavens, and the Highest gave his voice; hail stones and coals of fire.

Yea, he sent out his arrows, and scattered them; and he shot out lightnings, and discomfited them.

Then the channels of waters were seen, and the foundations of the world were discovered at thy rebuke, O Lord, at the blast of the breath of thy nostrils.

He sent from above, he took me, he drew me out of many waters.

He delivered me from my strong enemy, and from them which hated me: for they were too strong for me.

They prevented me in the day of my calamity: but the Lord was my stay.

He brought me forth also into a large place; he delivered me, because he delighted in me.

The Lord rewarded me according to my righteousness; according to the cleanness of my hands hath he recompensed me.

For I have kept the ways of the Lord, and have not wickedly departed from my God.

For all his judgments were before me, and I did not put away his statutes from me.

I was also upright before him, and I kept myself from mine iniquity.

Therefore hath the Lord recompensed me according to my righteousness, according to the cleanness of my hands in his eyesight.

With the merciful thou wilt show thyself; with an upright man thou wilt show thyself upright;

With the pure thou wilt show thyself pure; and with the froward thou wilt show thyself froward.

For thou wilt save the afflicted people; but wilt bring down high looks.

For thou wilt light my candle: the Lord my God will enlighten my darkness.

For by thee I have run through a troop; and by my god have I leaped over a wall.

As for God, his way is perfect: the word of the Lord is tried: he is a buckler to all those that trust in him.

For who is God save the Lord? or who is a rock save our God?

It is God that girdeth me with strength, and maketh my way perfect.

He maketh my feet like hinds' feet, and setteth me upon my high places.

He teacheth my hands to war, so that a bow of steel is broken by mine arms.

Thou hast enlarged my steps under me, that my feet did not slip.

I have pursued mine enemies, and overtaken them: neither did I turn again till they were consumed.

I have wounded them that they were not able to rise: they are fallen under my feet.

For thou hast girded me with strength unto the battle: thou hast subdued under me those that repose up against me.

Thou hast also given me the necks of mine enemies; that I might destroy them that hate me.

They cried, but there was none to save them: even unto the Lord, but he answered them not.

Then did I beat them small as the dust before the wind: I did cast them out as the dirt in the streets.

Thou hast delivered me from the strivings of the people; and thou hast made me the head of the heathen: a people whom I have not known shall serve me.

As soon as they hear of me, they shall obey me: the strangers shall submit themselves unto me.

The strangers shall fade away, and be afraid out of their close places.

The Lord liveth; and blessed by my rock; and let the God of my salvation be exalted.

It is God that avengeth me, and subdueth the people under me.

He delivereth me from mine enemies: yea, thou liftest me up above those that rise up against me: thou hast delivered me from the violent man.

Therefore will I give thanks unto thee, O Lord, among the heathen, and sing praises unto thy name.

Great deliverance giveth he to his king; and showeth mercy to his anointed, to David and to his seed for evermore.

The next step is to perform the Mass of the Holy Ghost at midnight on the first Monday of the month. Presumably this implies that the earlier devotions should be done late the previous month. As an alternate, one could perform this with the phases of the moon, the Mass being performed either at the full or new moon.

(What follows is a Latin version of the ordinary Mass, edited for brevity and for the use of a solitary practitioner.)

The Latin Mass

The celebrant makes reverence to the altar and makes the sign of the cross, saying:

In nomine Patris, et Filii, et Spiritus Sancti. Amen.

Then with folded hands he says:

Introibo ad altare Dei.
Ad Deum qui laetificat iuventutem meam.
Adiutorium nostrum in nomine Domini. Qui fecit caelum et terram.

Bowing, he confesses:

Confiteor Deo omnipotenti, beatae Mariae semper Virgini, beato Michaeli Archangelo, beato Ioanni Baptistae, sanctis Apostolis Petro et Paulo, omnibus sanctis, et vobis, fratres: Auia peccavi nimis cogitatione, verbo et opere: [He strikes his breast three times] mea culpa, mea culpa, mea maxima culpa, Ideo precor beatam Mariam semper Virginem, beatum michaelem Archangelum, beatum Ioannem Baptistam, sanctos Apostolos Petrum et Paulum, omnes sanctos, et vos, fratres, orare pro me ad Dominum Deum nostrum.

He makes the sign of the cross and says:

Indulgentiam, absolutionem, et remissionem peccatorum nostrum tribuat nobis omnipotens et misericors Dominus. Amen.

He bows.

Deus, tu conversus vivificabis nos. Et plebs tua laetabitur in te. Ostende nobis, Domine, misericordiam tuam. Et salutare tuum da nobis. Domine, exaudi orationem meam. Et clamor meus ad te veniat. Dominus vobiscum. Et cum spiritu tuo.

He places joined hands on the altar, and bows, saying:

Oramus te, Domine, per merita Sanctorum tuorum, [kisses altar] quorum reliquiae hic sunt, et omnium Sanctorum: ut indulgere digneris omnia peccata mea. Amen.

He blesses the incense:

Ab illo bene [makes cross] dicaris, in cuius honore cremaberis. Amen.

He incenses the altar.

Kyrie, eleison. Kyrie, eleison. Kyrie, eleison. Christe, eleison, Christe, eleison. Christe, eleison. Kyrie, eleison. Kyrie eleison. Kyrie, eleison.
Gloria in excelsis Deo it in terra pax hominibus bonae voluntatis. Laudzmus te, Benedicimus te. Adoramus te. Glorificamus te. Gratias agimus tibi propter magnam gloriam tuam. Domine Deus, Rex caelstis, Deus Pater omnipotens. Domine fili unigenite, Iesu Christe. Domine Deus, Agnus Dei, filius Patris. Qui tollis peccata mundi, miserere nobis. Qui tollis peccata mundi, suscipe depracationem nostram, Qui sedes ad dexteram Patris, miserere nobis. Quoniam tu solus sanctus. Tu solus Dominus. Tu solus Altissimus, Iesu Christe, cum Sancto Spiritu: in gloria Dei Patris. Amen.

Bow once more to the altar saying:

Munda cor meum Iube, domine, benedicere. Dominus sit in corde meo et in labiis meis: ut digne et competenter annuntiem Evangelium suum. Amen.

Then:

Credo in unum Deum. Patrem omnipotentem, factorem caeli et terrae, im visibilium omnium et invisibilium et in unum Dominum Iesum Christum, Filium Dei unigentium. Et ex Patre natum ante omnia saecula. Deum de Deo, lumen de lumine, Deum verum de Deo vero. Gentum, non factum, consubstantialem Patri: per quem omnia facta sunt. Qui propter nos homines et propter nostram salutem descendit de caelis. Et incarnatus est de Spiritu Sancto ex Maria Virgine: et homo factus est. Crucifixus etiam pro nobis: sub Pontio Pilato passus, et sepultus est. Et resurrexit tertia die, secundum Scripturas. Et ascendit in caelum: sedet ad dexteram Patris. Wt iterum venturus ext cum gloria iudicare vivos et mortuos: cuius regni non erit finis. Et in Spiritum Sanctum, Dominum, et vivificantem: qui ex Patre et Filio simul adoratur et conglorificatur: qui locutus ext per Prophetas, Et unam sanctam catholicam et apostolicam Ecclesiam. Confiteor unum baptisma in remissionem peccatorum. Et expecto resurrectionem mortuorum. Et vitam venturi saeculi. Amen.

The priest takes the host, and offers it, saying:

Suscipe, sancte Pater, omnipotens aeterne Deus, hanc immaculatam hostiam, quam ego indignus famnulus tuus offero tibi Deo meo, vivo et vero, pro innumerabilibus peccatis, et offensionibus, et negligentiis meis, et pro omnibus circumstantibus, sed et pro omnibus fidelibus christianis vivis atque defunctis: ut mihi et illis proficiat ad salutem in vitam aeternam. Amen.

He makes a cross with the host and paten and places them upon the altar. Then he pours the wine into the chalice and makes the sign of the cross over it saying:

Deus, qui himanae substantiae dignitatem mirabiliter condidisti, et mirabilius reformasti: da nobis, per huius aquae et vini mysterium, eius divinitatis esse consortes, qui himanitatis nbostrae fieri dignatus est particeps, Iesus Christus, Filius tuus, Dominus noster: Qui tecum vivit et regnat in unitate Spiritus Sancti, Deus, per omnia saecula saeculorum. Amen.

He lifts the chalice and offers it, saying:

Offerimus tibi, domine, calicem salutaris, tuam deprecantes clementiam: ut in conspectu divinae maiestatis tuae, pro nostra et totius mundi salute, cum odore suavitatis ascendat. Amen.

He makes the sign of the cross with the chalice.

He takes the host, holds it above the chalice, and breaks it in two, saying:

Per eundem Dominum nostrum Iesum Christum, filium tuum.

After the consecration of the Host (hosts can be purchased at Catholic supply stores, or the Sexual ritual may be used) it is held in the left hand and the operator, on his knees, says:

My Sovereign Savior Jesus Christ, Son of the Living God! Thou Who for the Salvation of all mankind didst suffer the death of the Cross; Thou Who, before being abandoned to Thine enemies, by an impulse of ineffable love, didst institute the Sacrament of Thy Body; Thou Who hast vouchsafed to us miserable creatures the privilege of making daily commemoration thereof; do Thou deign unto Thine unworthy servant, thus holding Thy Living Body in his hands, all strength and ability for the profitable application of that power with which he has been entrusted against the horde of rebellious spirits. Thou art their true God, and if they tremble at the utterance of Thy Name, upon that Holy Name will I call, crying Jesus Christ! Jesus, be Thou my help now and forever! Amen.

He consumes the consecrated wine and host. When the next mass is said, the wine and host are saved for use in magic.

The magician may rest until sunrise, at which time a black cock must be killed, and the first feather of its left wing plucked out and saved for later use. The eyes, tongue and heart must be torn out. These must also be saved and dried in the sun to be ground into powder. The carcass must be buried the following sunset in a secret place, a cross a palm in height being set upon the mound. At each of the four corners of the cross these signs must be drawn in the air with the thumb:

$$\text{B } \gamma \leftrightarrow 9 + 2 \; \text{Z} \; 1$$

The operator must eat no meat and consume no alcohol from the time of the sacrifice until its burial.

On the following day, at dawn, the operator says another Mass, placing the wing feather from the cock on the altar, together with a new unused penknife.

The magician now uses the knife to make a quill pen from the wing feather. Dipping it in the consecrated wine, he writes the following on a clean sheet of paper:

$$\bigvee I \; Z \; T \; \omega$$

This paper, some of the wine, and the host should be wrapped in a violet silk cloth and set aside.

On Thursday, the magician rises at midnight and lights a yellow taper inscribed with the sign of the cross. He then reads:

Psalm 78:

Give ear, O my people, to my law: incline your ears to the words of my mouth.

I will open my mouth in a parable: I will utter dark sayings of old:

Which we have heard and known, and our fathers have told us.

We will not hide them from their children, showing to the generation to come the praises of the LORD, and his strength, and his wonderful works that he hath done.

For he established a testimony in Jacob, and appointed a law in Israel, which he commanded our fathers, that they should make them known to their children:

That the generation to come might know them, even the children which should be born; who should arise and declare them to their children:

That they might set their hope in God, and not forget the works of God, but keep his commandments:

And might not be as their fathers, a stubborn and rebellious generation; a generation that set not their heart aright, and whose spirit was not steadfast with God.

The children of Ephraim, being armed, and carrying bows, turned back in the day of battle.

They kept not the covenant of God, and refused to walk in his law;

And forgot his works, and his wonders that he had showed them.

Marvelous things did he in the sight of their fathers, in the land of Egypt, in the field of Zoan.

He divided the sea, and caused them to pass through; and he made the waters to stand as an heap.

In the daytime also he led them with a cloud, and all the night with a light of fire.

He clave the rocks in the wilderness, and gave them drink as out of the great depths.

He brought streams also out of the rock, and caused waters to run down like rivers.

And they sinned yet more against him by provoking the most High in the wilderness. And they tempted God in their heart by asking meat for their lust.

Yea, they spake against God; they said, Can God furnish a table in the wilderness?

Behold, he smote the rock, that the waters gushed out, and the streams overflowed; can he give bread also? can he provide flesh for his people?

Therefore the LORD heard this, and was wroth: so a fire was kindled against Jacob, and anger also came up against Israel;

Because they believed not in God, and trusted not in his salvation:

Though he had commanded the clouds from above, and opened the doors of heaven,

And had rained down manna upon them to eat, and had given them of the corn of heaven.

Man did eat angel's food: he sent them meat to the full.

He caused an east wind to blow in the heaven: and by his power he brought in the south wind.

He rained flesh also upon them as dust, and feathered fowls like as the sand of the sea:

And he let it fall in the midst of their camp, round about their habitations.

So they did eat, and were well filled: for he gave them their own desire;

They were not estranged from their lust. But while their meat was yet in their mouths,

The wrath of God came upon them, and slew the fattest of them, and smote down the chosen men of Israel.

For all this they sinned still, and believed not for his wondrous works.

Therefore their days did he consume in vanity, and their years in trouble.

When he slew them, then they sought him: and they returned and inquired early after God.

And they remembered that God was their rock, and the high God their redeemer.

Nevertheless they did flatter him with their mouth, and they lied unto him with their tongues.

For their heart was not right with him, neither were they stedfast in his covenant.

But he, being full of compassion, forgave their iniquity, and destroyed them not: yea, many a time turned he his anger away, and did not stir up all his wrath.

For he remembered that they were but flesh; a wind that passeth away, and cometh not again.

How oft did they provoke him in the wilderness, and grieve him in the desert!

Yea, they turned back and tempted God, and limited the Holy One of Israel.

They remembered not his hand, nor the day when he delivered them from the enemy.

How he had wrought his signs in Egypt, and his wonders in the field of Zoan:

And had turned their rivers into blood; and their floods, that they could not drink.

He sent divers sorts of flies among them, which devoured them; and frogs, which destroyed them.

He gave also their increase unto the caterpillar, and their labour unto the locust.

He destroyed their vines with hail, and their sycamore trees with frost.

He gave up their cattle also to the hail, and their flocks to hot thunderbolts.

He cast upon them the fierceness of his anger, wrath, and indignation, and trouble, by sending evil angels among them.

He made a way to his anger; he spared not their soul from death, but gave their life over to the pestilence;

And smote all the firstborn in Egypt; the chief of their strength in the tabernacles of Ham:

But made his own people to go forth like sheep, and guided them in the wilderness like a flock.

And he led them on safely, so that they feared not: but the sea overwhelmed their enemies.

And he brought them to the border of his sanctuary, even to this mountain, which his right hand had purchased.

He cast out the heathen also before them, and divided them an inheritance by line, and made the tribes of Israel to dwell in their tents.

Yet they tempted and provoked the most high God, and kept not his testimonies:

But turned back, and dealt unfaithfully like their fathers: they were turned aside like a deceitful bow.

For they provoked him to anger with their high places, and moved him to jealousy with their graven images.

When God heard this, he was wroth, and greatly abhorred Israel:

So that he forsook the tabernacle of Shiloh, the tent which he placed among men;

And delivered his strength into captivity, and his glory into the enemy's hand.

He gave his people over also unto the sword; and was wroth with his inheritance.

The fire consumed their young men; and their maidens were not given to marriage.

Their priests fell by the sword; and their widows made no lamentation.

Then the Lord awaked as one out of sleep, and like a mighty man that shouteth by reason of wine.

And he smote his enemies in the hinder parts: he put them to a perpetual reproach.

Moreover he refused the tabernacle of Joseph, and chose not the tribe of Ephraim:

But chose the tribe of Judah, the mount Zion which he loved.

And he built his sanctuary like high palaces, like the earth which he hath established for ever.

He chose David also his servant, and took him from the sheepfolds:

From following the ewes great with young he brought him to feed Jacob his people, and Israel his inheritance.

So he fed them according to the integrity of his heart; and guided them by the skillfulness of his hands.

And then he reads:

Deliver us, O Lord, from the fear of hell. Let not the demons destroy my soul when I shall raise them from the deep pit, when I shall command them to do my will. May the day be bright, may the sun and moon shine forth, when I shall call upon them. Terrible of aspect are they, deformed and horrible to sight; but do Thou restore unto them their angelic shapes when I shall impose my will upon them. O Lord, deliver me from those of the dread visage, and grant that they shall be obedient when I shall raise them up from hell, when I shall impose my will for a law upon them.

After this the operator extinguishes the taper and, at sunrise, cuts the throat of a male lamb, taking care that the blood does not hit the earth. He then skins the lamb, saving the carcass (freezing is recommended) and burns the heart and tongue. The ashes are saved for later use. The skin of the lamb shall be spread in the middle of the field (or some more practical place), cleaned, and the process of curing begun, and sprinkled four times a day with holy water for nine days. On the tenth day, before the rising of the sun, the lambskin shall be covered with the ashes of the heart and tongue, and with the powdered organs of the cock.

On the following day, after sunset, the carcass of the lamb shall be buried in a hidden spot, safe from scavengers, and the operator with his thumb shall inscribe, either in the earth itself, or the air above the grave:

$$\mathsf{[} \sim \mathsf{L} \, 2 \, \mathsf{3} \, \mathsf{3} \, \mathsf{3}$$

For three days, he shall sprinkle the four corners of the grave with holy water saying:

Sprinkle me, O Lord, with hyssop, and I shall be cleansed! Wash me, and I shall be made whiter than snow!

Then, kneeling and facing east recite:

Christ Jesus, Redeemer of men, Who, being the Lamb without spot, wast immolated for the salvation of the human race, Who alone wast found worthy to open the

*Book of Life, impart such virtue to this lambskin that it may
receive the signs which we shall trace thereon, written with
thy blood, so that the figures, signs and words may become
efficacious; and grant that this skin may preserve us
against the wiles of the demons; that they may be terrified
at the sight of these figures and may only approach them
trembling. Through Thee, Jesus Christ, Who livest and
reignest through all ages. So be it.*

Then say:

*Immolated Lamb, be Thou a pillar of strength against the
demons! Slain Lamb, give power over the Powers of Darkness! Immolated Lamb, grant favor and strength unto the
binding of the Rebellious Spirits. So be it.*

Finish curing the lambskin and remove the fleece. Burn
the fleece and bury it with the carcass. Write the word
VELLUS in the earth above the grave, as well as the words:

*May this which hath been reduced to ashes preserve
against the demons through the name of Jesus.*

Below this write the following symbols:

And beneath this:

Set the lambskin on the eastern side of the grave and cut
into it these characters with a new knife:

Then recite *Psalm 71*:

In thee, O LORD, do I put my trust: let me never be put to confusion.

Deliver me in thy righteousness, and cause me to escape: incline thine ear unto me, and save me.

Be thou my strong habitation, whereunto I may continually resort: thou hast given commandment to save me; for thou art my rock and my fortress.

Deliver me, O my God, out of the hand of the wicked, out of the hand of the unrighteous and cruel man.

For thou art my hope, O Lord GOD: thou art my trust from my youth.

By thee have I been holden up from the womb: thou art he that took me out of my mother's bowels: my praise shall be continually of thee.

I am as a wonder unto many; but thou art my strong refuge.

Let my mouth be filled with thy praise and with thy honour all the day.

Cast me not off in the time of old age; forsake me not when my strength faileth.

For mine enemies speak against me; and they that lay wait for my soul take counsel together,

Saying, God hath forsaken him: persecute and take him; for there is none to deliver him.

O God, be not far from me: O my God, make haste for my help.

Let them be confounded and consumed that are adversaries to my soul; let them be covered with reproach and dishonour that seek my hurt.

But I will hope continually, and will yet praise thee more and more.

My mouth shall show forth thy righteousness and thy salvation all the day; for I know not the numbers thereof.

I will go in the strength of the Lord GOD: I will make mention of thy righteousness, even of thine only.

O God, thou hast taught me from my youth: and hitherto have I declared thy wondrous works.

Now also when I am old and greyheaded, O God, forsake me not; until I have showed thy strength unto this generation, and thy power to every one that is to come.

Thy righteousness also, O God, is very high, who hast done great things: O God, who is like unto thee!

Thou, which hast showed me great and sore troubles, shalt quicken me again, and shalt bring me up again from the depths of the earth.

Thou shalt increase my greatness, and comfort me on every side.

I will also praise thee with the psaltery, even thy truth, O my God: unto thee will I sing with the harp, O thou Holy One of Israel.

My lips shall greatly rejoice when I sing unto thee; and my soul, which thou hast redeemed.

My tongue also shall talk of thy righteousness all the day long: for they are confounded, for they are brought unto shame, that seek my hurt.

Cut the following symbols into the skin:

Then recite *Psalm 95*:

O come, let us sing unto the LORD: let us make a joyful noise to the rock of our salvation.

Let us come before his presence with thanksgiving, and make a joyful noise unto him with psalms.

For the LORD is a great God, and a great King above all gods.

In his hand are the deep places of the earth: the strength of the hills is his also.

The sea is his, and he made it: and his hands formed the dry land.

O come, let us worship and bow down: let us kneel before the LORD our maker.

For he is our God; and we are the people of his pasture, and the sheep of his hand. To day if ye will hear his voice,

Harden not your heart, as in the provocation, and as in the day of temptation in the wilderness:

When your fathers tempted me, proved me, and saw my work.

Forty years long was I grieved with this generation, and said, It is a people that do err in their heart, and they have not known my ways:

Unto whom I swear in my wrath that they should not enter into my rest.

And cut into the skin:

Next recite *Psalm 77:*

I cried unto God with my voice, even unto God with my voice; and he gave ear unto me.

In the day of my trouble I sought the Lord: my sore ran in the night, and ceased not: my soul refused to be comforted.

I remembered God, and was troubled: I complained, and my spirit was overwhelmed. Selah.

Thou holdest mine eyes waking: I am so troubled that I cannot speak.

I have considered the days of old, the years of ancient times.

I call to remembrance my song in the night: I commune with mine own heart: and my spirit made diligent search.

Will the Lord cast off for ever? and will he be favourable no more?

Is his mercy clean gone for ever? doth his promise fail for evermore?

Hath God forgotten to be gracious? hath he in anger shut up his tender mercies? Selah.

And I said, This is my infirmity: but I will remember the years of the right hand of the most High.

I will remember the works of the LORD: surely I will remember thy wonders of old.

I will meditate also of all thy work, and talk of thy doings.

Thy way, O God, is in the sanctuary: who is so great a God as our God?

Thou art the God that doest wonders: thou hast declared thy strength among the people.

Thou hast with thine arm redeemed thy people, the sons of Jacob and Joseph. Selah.

The waters saw thee, O God, the waters saw thee; they were afraid: the depths also were troubled.

The clouds poured out water: the skies sent out a sound: thine arrows also went abroad.

The voice of thy thunder was in the heaven: the lightnings lightened the world: the earth trembled and shook.

Thy way is in the sea, and thy path in the great waters, and thy footsteps are not known.

Thou leadest thy people like a flock by the hand of Moses and Aaron.

And carve the following:

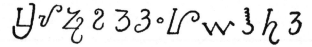

Then recite *Psalm 2*:

Why do the heathen rage, and the people imagine a vain thing?

The kings of the earth set themselves, and the rulers take counsel together, against the LORD, and against his anointed, saying,

Let us break their bands asunder, and cast away their cords from us.

He that sitteth in the heavens shall laugh: the Lord shall have them in derision.

Then shall he speak unto them in his wrath, and vex them in his sore displeasure.

Yet have I set my king upon my holy hill of Zion.

I will declare the decree: the LORD hath said unto me, Thou art my Son; this day have I begotten thee.

Ask of me, and I shall give thee the heathen for thine inheritance, and the uttermost parts of the earth for thy possession.

Thou shalt break them with a rod of iron; thou shalt dash them in pieces like a potter's vessel.

Be wise now therefore, O ye kings: be instructed, ye judges of the earth.

Serve the LORD with fear, and rejoice with trembling.

Kiss the Son, lest he be angry, and ye perish from the way, when his wrath is kindled but a little. Blessed are all they that put their trust in him.

And then cut:

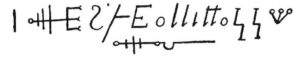

Then recite *Psalm 115*:

Not unto us, O LORD, not unto us, but unto thy name give glory, for thy mercy, and for thy truth's sake.

Wherefore should the heathen say, Where is now their God?

But our God is in the heavens: he hath done whatsoever he hath pleased.

Their idols are silver and gold, the work of men's hands.

They have mouths, but they speak not: eyes have they, but they see not:

They have ears, but they hear not: noses have they, but they smell not:

They have hands, but they handle not: feet have they, but they walk not: neither speak they through their throat.

They that make them are like unto them; so is every one that trusteth in them.

O Israel, trust thou in the LORD: he is their help and their shield.

O house of Aaron, trust in the LORD: he is their help and their shield.

Ye that fear the LORD, trust in the LORD: he is their help and their shield.

The LORD hath been mindful of us: he will bless us; he will bless the house of Israel; he will bless the house of Aaron.

He will bless them that fear the LORD, both small and great.

The LORD shall increase you more and more, you and your children.

Ye are blessed of the LORD which made heaven and earth.

The heaven, even the heavens, are the LORD's: but the earth hath he given to the children of men.

The dead praise not the LORD, neither any that go down into silence.

But we will bless the LORD from this time forth and for evermore. Praise the LORD.

Then say:

In Honor of the Most Holy and August Trinity, the Father, the Son, and the Holy Ghost. Amen.

Trinitas, Sother, Messias, Emmanuel, Sabahot, Adonay, Athanatos, Jesu, Pentagna, Agragon, Ischiros, Eleyson, Otheos, Tetragrammaton, Ely, Saday, Aquila, Magnus Homo, Visio, Flos, Origo, Salvator, Alpha and Omega, Primus, Novissimus, Principium et Finis, Primogenitus, Sapientia, Virtus, Paraclitus, Veritas, Via, Mediator, Medicus, Salus, Agnus, Ovis, Vitulus, Spes, Aries, Leo, Lux, Imago, Panis, Janua, Petra, Sponsa, Pastor, Propheta, Sacerdos, Sanctus, Immortalitas, Jesus, Christus, Pater Filius Hominis, Sanctus, Pater Omnipotens, Deus, Agios, Resurrectio, Mischiros, Charitas, Aeternas, Creator, Redemptor, Unitas, Summum Bonum, Infinitas. Amen.

[The seventy-two great names of God.]

The finished skin is the magician's principal badge of power, along with the pentacles. He is to have it with him during all conjurations as a shield of protection and emblem of authority.

Here follow the four pentacles to be used to compel the demons, and for defense:

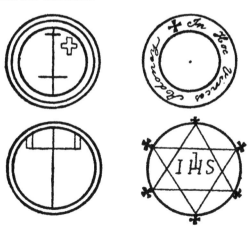

Read the Gospel according to John, to the fourteenth verse. Then:

Thanks be to God. Hosanna to the Son of David! Blessed is He Who Cometh in the Name of the Lord. Hosanna in the Highest. We invoke Thee, O blessed and glorious Trinity! May the Name of the Lord be blessed, now and henceforth for ever! Amen. In the Name of the Father, of the Son and of the Holy Ghost, Jesus of Nazareth, King of the Jews. May Christ conquer ✠ reign ✠ command ✠ and defend me from all evil. Amen.

UNIVERSAL CONJURATION

I, [name] do conjure thee, O spirit N… by the living God, by the true God, by the holy and all-ruling god, Who created from nothingness the heaven, the earth, the sea and all things that are therein, in virtue of the Most Holy Sacrament of the Eucharist, in the name of Jesus Christ, and by the power of this same Almighty Son of God, Who for us and for our redemption was crucified, suffered death and was buried; Who rose again on the third day and is now seated on the right hand of the Creator of the whole world, from whence He will come to judge the living and dead; as also by the precious love of the Holy Spirit, perfect Trinity. I conjure thee within the circle, accursed one, by thy judgment, who didst dare to tempt God: I exorcise thee, Serpent, and I command thee to appear forthwith under a beautiful and well-favored human form of soul and body, and to fulfill my behest without any deceit whatsoever as also without mental reservation of any kind, by the great Names of the God of gods and Lord of lords, Adonay, Tetragrammaton, Jehova, Otheos, Athanatos, Ischyros, Agla, Pentagrammaton, Saday, Saday, Saday, Jehova, Otheos, Athanatos, Sady, Sady, Sady, Cados, Cados, Cados, Eloy Agla, Agla, Agla, Adonay, Adonay. I conjure thee, Evil and Accursed Serpent, N…, to appear at my will and pleasure, in this place, before this circle, without tarrying, without companions, without grievance, without noise, deformity or murmuring. I exorcise thee by the ineffable Names of God, to wit, Gog and Magog, which I am unworthy to pronounce: Come hither, Come hither, Come hither. Accomplish my will and desire, without wile or falsehood. Otherwise St. Michael, the invisible Archangel, shall presently blast thee in the utmost depths of hell. Come, then, N…, to do my will.

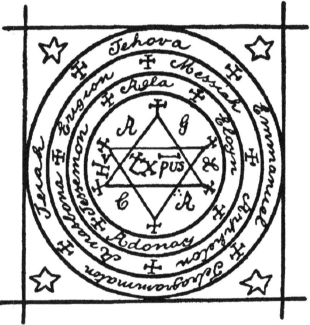

The Grand Pentacle of Solomon
For Use In Commanding The Spirits

Compulsion Of The Demon

Why tarriest thou, and why delayest? What doest thou? Make ready, obey thy master, in the name of the Lord, Bathat or Rachat flowing over Abracmens, Alchor over Aberer.

If the demon does not appear, uncover the Pentacle saying:

Command Of The Pentacle

Behold the Pentacle of Solomon which I have brought into thy presence! I command thee, by order of the great God, Adonay, Tetragrammaton and Jesus! Hasten, fulfill my behests, without wile or falsehood, but in all truth, in the name of the Savior and Redeemer, Jesus Christ.

Discharge To The Spirit

Go in peace unto your places. May there be peace between us and you, and be ye ready to come when ye are called. In the Name of the Father, and of the Son, and of the Holy Ghost. Amen.

Thanksgiving

Praise, honor, glory and blessing be unto Him Who sitteth upon the throne, Who liveth for ever and ever. Amen.

THE LIBER SPIRITUUM

The magician, to further his hold over the demons, will obtain or make a book with blank pages, for the purpose of compelling the demons to sign it (that is, give a personal sign or sigil in a vision) binding them in mutual agreement with the operator. After this, they can be called by the magus without lengthy ceremony.

The book, once made, is to be consecrated by reciting:

Conjuration Of The Book

I conjure thee, O Book, to be useful and profitable unto all who shall have recourse to thee for the success of their affairs. I conjure thee anew, by the virtue of the Blood of Jesus Christ, contained daily in the chalice, to be service-able unto all those who shall read thee. I exorcise thee, in the Name of the Most Holy Trinity, in the Name of the Most Holy Trinity, in the name of the Most Holy Trinity!

After the book has been consecrated and begun to be used, it must be sealed. This must be said before the sealing of the book:

I conjure and command you, O Spirits, all and so many as ye are, to accept this Book with good grace, so that whensoever we may read it, the same being approved and recognized as in proper form and valid, you shall be constrained to appear in comely human form when you are called, accordingly as the reader shall judge. In no circumstances shall you make any attempt upon the body, soul or spirit of the reader, nor inflict any harm on those who may accompany him, either by mutterings, tempests, noise, scandals, nor yet by lesion or by hindrance in the execution of the commands of this Book. I conjure you to appear immediately when the conjuration is made, to execute without dallying all that is written and enumerated in its proper place in the said book. You shall obey, serve, instruct, impart and perform all in your power for the benefit of those who command you, and the whole without illusion. If perchance some of the invoked spirits be unable to come or appear when required, they shall be bound over to send others vested with their power, who also shall swear solemnly to execute all that the reader may demand, and ye are all hereby enjoined by the Most holy Names of the Omnipotent Living God, Eloym, Jah, El, Eloy, Tetragrammaton, to fulfill everything as it is set forth above. If ye obey me not, I will force you to abide in torments for a thousand years, as also if any one of you receive not the Book with entire resignation to the will of the reader.

Conjuration Of The Demons, For Use With The Book

In the name of the Father, and of the Son, and of the Holy Ghost. Take heed! Come, all Spirits! By the virtue and power of your King, by the seven crowns and chains of your Kings, all Spirits of the Hells are forced to appear in my presence before this pentacle or circle of Solomon, whensoever I shall call them. Come, then, all at my orders, to fulfill that which is in your power, as commanded. Come, therefore, from the East, South, West, and North! I conjure and command you, by the virtue and power of Him Who is three, eternal, equal, Who is God invisible, consubstantial, in a word, Who has created the heavens, the sea and all which is under heaven.

When the demons appear, command them to give you a controlling sigil to fix in the book, along with it's powers and areas of authority.

THE CIRCLE OF EVOCATION

The circle must be laid down, according to Pope Honorius, in charcoal and holy water. For the modern practitioner, this says that it must be in some physical form, and be cleansed and consecrated.

The circle should be fashioned according to the pattern of Honorius here given:

What Must Be Said In Composing The Circle

O Lord, we fly to Thy virtue! O Lord, confirm this work! What is operated in us becomes like dust driven before the wind, and the Angel of the Lord pausing, let the darkness disappear, and the Angel of the Lord ever pursuing, Alpha, Omega, Ely, Elohe, Elohim, Zabahot, Elion, Sady. Behold the Lion Who is the conqueror of the Tribe of Juday, the Root of David! I will open the Book, and the seven seals thereof. I have beheld Satan as a bolt falling from heaven. It is Thou Who hast given us power to crush dragons, scorpions and all Thine enemies beneath Thy feet. Nothing shall harm us, not even Eloy, Elohim, Elohe, Zabahot, Elion, Esarchie, Adonay, Jah, Tetragrammaton, Sady. The earth is the Lord's and all those who dwell therein, because He established it upon the seas and prepared it in the midst of the waves. Who shall ascend unto the mountain of the Lord? Who shall be received in his Holy Place? The innocent of hands and clean of heart. Who hath not received his soul in vain and hath not sworn false witness against his neighbor. The same shall be blessed of God and shall obtain mercy of God to his salvation. He is of the generation of these who seek Him. Open your gates, ye princes, open the eternal gates, and the King of Glory shall enter! Who is this King of Glory? The Lord Almighty, the Lord, mighty in battle. Open your gates, ye princes! Lift up the eternal gates. Who is this King of Glory? The Lord Almighty. This Lord is the King of Glory. Glory be to the Father, the Son and the Holy Spirit.

CONJURATION OF THE DEMON KINGS

Conjuration Of The King Of The East

I conjure and invoke thee, O powerful King of the East, Magoa, by my holy labor, by all the names of Divinity, by the name of the All-Powerful: I command thee to obey, and to come to me, or that failing, forthwith and immediately to send unto me Massayel, Ariel, Satiel, Arduel, Acorib, to respond concerning all that I would know and to fulfill all that I shall command. Else thou shalt come verily in thine own person, to satisfy my will; which refusing, I shall compel thee by all the virtue and power of God.

The Grand Pentacle or Circle of Solomon will answer for the above and following conjurations, which can be said on all days and at all hours. If it be desired to speak only with one spirit, one only need be named.

Conjuration Of The King Of The South

O Egym, great King of the South, I conjure and invoke thee by the most high and holy Names of God, do thou here manifest, clothed with all thy power; come before this circle, or at least send me forthwith Fadal, Nastrache, to make answer unto me, and to execute all my wishes. If thou failest, I shall force thee by God Himself.

Conjuration Of The King Of The West

O Baymon, most potent King, who reignest in the Western quarter, I call and I invoke thee in the name of the Deity! I command thee by virtue of the Most High, to send me immediately before this circle the spirit Passiel Rosus, with all other spirits who are subject unto thee, that the same may answer in everything, even as I shall require them. If thou failest, I will torment thee with the sword of fire divine; I will multiply thy sufferings and will burn thee.

Conjuration Of The King Of The North

(Note that this conjuration is longest because the northern quarter is traditionally the most evil and therefore the most demonically powerful.)

O thou, Amaymon, King and Emperor of the Northern parts, I call, invoke, exorcise and conjure thee, by the virtue and power of the Creator, and by the virtue of virtues, to send me presently, and without delay, Madael, Laaval, Bamlahe, Belem and Ramath, with all other spirits of thine obedience, in comely and human form! In whatsoever place thou now art, come hither and render that honor which thou owest to the true living God, Who is thy Creator. In the name of the Father, of the Son and of the Holy Ghost, come therefore, and be obedient, in front of this circle, without peril to my body or soul. Appear in comely human form, with no terror encompassing thee. I conjure thee, make haste, come straightway, and at once. By all the Divine names—Sechiel, Barachiel—if thou dost not obey promptly, Balandier, suspensus, iracundus, Origratiumgu, Partus, Olemdemis, and Bautratis, N... I exorcise thee do invoke and do impose most high commandment upon thee, by the omnipotence of the living God, and of the true God; by the virtue of the holy God, and by the power of Him Who spake and all things were made, even by His holy commandment the heaven and earth were made, with all that is in them! I adjure thee by the Father, by the Son and by the Holy Ghost, even by the Holy Trinity, by that God Whom thou canst not resist, under Whose empire I will compel thee; I conjure thee by God the Father, by God the Son, by God the Holy Ghost, by the Mother of Jesus Christ, Holy Mother and perpetual Virgin, by her sacred heart, by her blessed milk, which the Son of the Father sucked, by her most holy body and soul, by all the parts and members of this Virgin, by all the sufferings, labors, agonies which she endured during the whole course of her life, by all the sighs she uttered, by all the holy tears which she shed whilst her dear Son wept before the time of His dolorous passion and on the tree of the Cross, by all the others, as in heaven so on earth, in honor of our Savior Jesus Christ, and of the Blessed Mary, His Mother, by whatsoever is celestial, by the Church Militant, in honor of the Virgin and of all the saints. In like manner, I conjure thee by the Holy Trinity, by all other mysteries, by the sign of the Cross, by the most precious blood and water which flowed from the side of Jesus Christ, by the sweat which issued from His whole body, when He said in the Garden of Olives: My Father, if it be possible, let this chalice pass from me. I conjure thee by His death and passion, by His burial and glorious resurrection, by His Ascension, by the coming of the Holy Ghost. I adjure thee, furthermore, by the crown of thorns which was set upon His head, by the blood which flowed from His feet and hands, by the nails with which He was nailed to the tree of the Cross, by the holy tears which He shed, by all which He suffered willingly through great love of us: by the lungs, the heart, the hair, the inward parts, and all the members of our Savior Jesus Christ. I conjure thee by the judgment of the living and the dead, by the Gospel words of our Savior Jesus Christ, by His preachings, by His sayings, by his miracles, by the child in swaddling clothes, by the crying child, borne by the mother in her most pure and virginal womb; by the glorious intercession of the Virgin Mother of our Savior Jesus Christ; by all which is of God and of His Most Holy Mother, as in heaven so on earth. I conjure thee by the holy Angels, and Archangels, by all the blessed orders of Spirits, by the holy patriarchs and prophets, by all the holy martyrs and confessors, by all the holy virgins and innocent widows, by all the saints of God, both men and women. I conjure thee by the head of St. John the Baptist, by the milk of St. Catherine, and by all the Saints.

Conjurations For Each Day Of The Week

For Monday, To Lucifer

This is performed within the proper circle (illustrated below) between eleven and twelve o'clock or between three and four. The operator must have coal and consecrated chalk to compose the circle, about which these words must be written:

I forbid thee Lucifer, in the name of the Most Holy Trinity, to enter within this circle.

A mouse must be provided as a sacrifice. The magician should have holy water, and be dressed in a stole, an alb, and surplice. He must recite the conjuration in a lively manner, commanding sharply and shortly, as a lord should address his servant, with all kinds of menaces:

Satan, Rantam, Pallantre, Lutais, Coricacoem, Scircigreur, I require thee to give me very humbly, etc.

Conjuration

I conjure thee, Lucifer, by the living God, by the true God, by the holy God, Who spake and all was made, Who commanded and all things were created and made! I conjure thee by the Ineffable Names of God, On, Alpha and Omega, Eloy, Eloym, Ya Saday, Lux, Mugiens, Rex Salus, Adonay, Emmanuel, Messias; and I adjure, conjure, and exorcise thee by the Names which are declared under the

letters V, C, X, as also by the names Jehovah, Sol, Agla,
Riffasoris, Oriston, Orphitne, Phaton irretu, Ogia,
Speraton, Imagon, Amul, Penaton, Soter, Tetragrammaton,
Eloy, Premoton, Sitmon, Periphaton, Simulaton, Perpi,
Klarimum, Tremendum, Meray, and by the most high
Ineffable Names of God, Gali, Enga, El, Habdanum,
Ingodum, Obu, Englabis, do thou make haste to come, or
send me N…, having a comely and human form, in no wise
repulsive, that he may answer in real truth whatsoever I
shall ask him, being also powerless to hurt me, or any
person whomsoever, either in body or soul.

For Tuesday, To Frimost

This is performed in its proper circle (see below) at night
from nine to ten o'clock, and the first stone found by the
magician is to be given as an offering. He is to be received
with dignity and honor. Proceed as on Monday. Compose
the circle and write about it: *Obey me, Frimost! Obey me,*
Frimost! Obey me, Frimost!

Conjuration

I conjure and command thee, Frimost, by all the names wherewith thou canst be constrained and bound! I exorcise thee Nambroth, by thy name, by the virtue of all spirits, by all characters, by the Jewish, Greek and Chaldean Conjurations, by thy confusion and malediction, and I will redouble thy pains and torments from day to day for ever, if thou come not now to accomplish my will and submit to all that I shall command being powerless to harm me, or those who accompany me, either in body or soul.

For Wednesday, To Astaroth

This is performed in its circle at night, from ten to eleven o'clock; it is designed to obtain the good graces of the King (presumably of France) and others. Write in the circle as follows: *Come, Astaroth! Come Astaroth! Come Astaroth!*

Conjuration

I conjure thee, Astaroth, wicked spirit, by the words and virtues of God, by the powerful God, Jesus Christ of Naza-

reth, unto Whom all demons are submitted, Who was conceived of the Virgin Mary; by the mystery of the Angel Gabriel, I conjure thee; and again in the name of the Father, and of the Son, and of the Holy Ghost; in the name of the glorious Virgin Mary and of the Most Holy Trinity, in Whose honor do all the Archangels, Thrones, Dominations, Powers, Patriarchs, Prophets, Apostles and Evangelists sing without end; Hosannah, Hosannah, Hosannah, Lord God of Hosts, Who art, Who wast, Who art to come, as a river of burning fire! Neglect not my commands, refuse not to come, I command thee by Him Who shall appear with flames to judge the living and the dead unto Whom is all honor, praise and glory. Come, therefore, promptly, obey my will; appear and give praise to the true God, unto the living God, yea, unto all his works; fail not to obey me, and give honor to the Holy Ghost, in Whose name I command thee.

For Thursday, To Silcharde

This is done in his circle, at night, from three to four o'clock, at which hour he is called, and appears in the form of a King. A little bread must be given him when he is required to depart; he renders man happy and also discovers treasures. Write about the circle as follows: *Holy God! Holy God! Holy God!*

Conjuration

I conjure thee, Silcharde, by the image and likeness of Jesus Christ our Savior, Whose death and passion redeemed the entire human race, Who also wills that, by His providence, thou appear forthwith in this place. I command thee by all the Kingdoms of God. I adjure and constrain thee by His Holy name, by Him Who walked upon the asp, Who crushed the lion and the dragon. Do thou obey me and fulfill my commands, being powerless to do harm unto me or any person whomsoever, either in body or soul.

For Friday, To Bechard

This is performed at night from eleven to twelve o'clock, and a nut must be given to him. Write within the circle: *Come, Bechard! Come, Bechard! Come, Bechard!*

Conjuration

I conjure thee, Bechard, and constrain thee, in like manner, by the Most Holy Names of God, Eloy, Adonay, Eloy, Agla, Samalabactay, which are written in Hebrew, Greek and Latin; by all the sacraments, by all the names written in this book; and by him who drove thee from the height of Heaven. I conjure and command thee by the virtue of the Most Holy Eucharist, which hath redeemed men from their sins; I conjure thee to come without any delay, to do and perform all my bidings, without any prejudice to my body or soul, without harming my book or doing injury to those that accompany me.

For Saturday, To Guland

This is performed at night from eleven to twelve o'clock, and so soon as he appears burnt bread must be given him. Ask him anything that you will, and he will obey you on the spot. Write in his circle: *Enter not, Guland! Enter not, Guland! Enter not, Guland!*

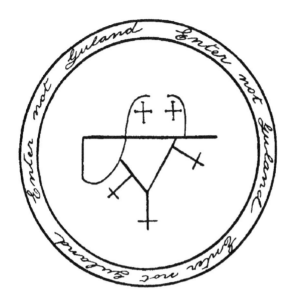

Conjuration

I conjure thee, O Guland, in the name of Satan, in the name of Beelzebub, in the name of Astaroth, and in the name of all other spirits, to make haste and appear before me. Come then, in the name of Satan and in the names of all other demons. Come to me, I command thee, in the Name of the Most Holy Trinity. Come without inflicting any harm upon me, without injury to my body or soul, without maltreating my books or anything which I use. I command thee to appear without delay, or that failing, to send me forthwith another Spirit having the same power as thou hast, who shall accomplish my commands and be submitted to my will, wanting which, he whom thou shalt send me, if indeed thou comest not thyself, shall in no wise depart, nor until he hath in all things fulfilled my desire.

For Sunday, To Surgat

This is performed at night from eleven to one o'clock. He will demand a hair of your head, but give him one of a fox, and see that he takes it. His office is to discover and transport all treasures and perform anything that you may will. Write in his circle: *Tetragrammaton, Tetragrammaton, Tetragrammaton. Ismael, Adonay, Ihua.* And in a second circle: *Come Surgat! Come Surgat! Come Surgat!*

Conjuration

I conjure thee, O Surgat, by all the names which are written in this book, to present thyself here before me, promptly and without delay, being ready to obey me in all things, or, failing this, to despatch me a spirit with a stone which shall make me invisible to every one whensoever I carry it! And I conjure thee to be submitted in thine own person, or in the person of him or of those whom thou shalt send me, and to accomplish my will and all that I shall command, without harm to me or to any one, so soon as I make known my intent.

VERY POWERFUL CONJURATION FOR
ALL DAYS & HOURS OF THE DAY OR NIGHT,
BEING FOR TREASURES HIDDEN BY MEN OR SPIRITS,
THAT THE SAME MAY BE POSSESSED & TRANSPORTED.

I command you, O all ye demons dwelling in these parts, or in what part of the world soever ye may be, by whatsoever power may have been given you by God and our holy Angels over this place, by the powerful Principality of the infernal abysses, as also by all your brethren, both general and special demons, whether dwelling in the East, West, South or North, demons, or in any side of the earth, and, in like manner, by the power of God the Father, by the wisdom of God the Son, by the virtue of the Holy Ghost, by the authority I derive from our Savior Jesus Christ, the only Son of the Almighty and the Creator Who Made us and all creatures from nothing, Who also ordains that you do thereby abdicate all power to guard, habit and abide in this place; by Whom further I constrain and command you nolens, volens, without guile or deception, to declare me your names and to leave me in peaceable possession and rule over this place of whatsoever legion you be and of whatsoever part of the world; by order of the Most Holy Trinity and by the merits of the Most Holy and Blessed Virgin, as also of all the saints, I unbind you all, spirits who abide in this place, and I drive you to the deepest infernal abysses. Thus: Go, all spirits accursed, who are condemned to the flame eternal which is prepared for you and your companions, if ye be rebellious and disobedient. I conjure you by the same authority, I exhort and call you, I constrain and command you, by all the powers of your superior demons, to come, obey and reply positively to what I direct you, in the Name of Jesus Christ. Whence, if you or they do not obey promptly and without tarrying I will shortly increase your torments for a thousand years in hell. I constrain you therefore to appear here in comely

*human shape, by the Most High Names of God, Hain, Lon,
Hilay, Sabaoth, Helim, Radisha, Ledieha, Adonay, Jehova,
Yah, Tetragrammaton, Sadai, Messias, Agios, Ischyros,
Emmanuel, Agla, Jesus Who is Alpha and Omega, the
beginning and the end, that you be justly established in the
fire having no power to reside, habit or abide in this place
henceforth; and I require your doom by the virtue of the
said Names, to wit that St. Michael drive you to the
uttermost of the infernal abyss, in the Name of the Father,
and of the Son, and of the Holy Ghost. So be it.*

*I conjure thee, Acham, or whomsoever thou mayest be, by
the Most Holy Names of God, by Malhame, Jae, May,
Mabron, Jacob, Dasmedias, Eloy, Aterestin, Janastardy,
Finis, Agios, Ischyros, Otheos, Athanatos, Agla, Jehova,
Homosion, Aga, Messias, Sother, Christus vincit, Christus
imperat, Increatus Spiritus Sanctus.*

*I conjure thee Cassiel, or whomsoever thou mayest be, by
all the said names, with power and with exorcism! I warn
thee by the other sacred Names of the most great Creator,
which are or shall hereafter be communicated to thee;
hearken forthwith and immediately to my words; observe
them inviolably, as sentences of the last dreadful day of
judgment, which thou must obey inviolately, nor think to
repulse me because I am a sinner, for therein shalt thou
repulse the commands of the Most High God. Knowest thou
not that thou art bereft of thy powers before thy Creator
and ours? Think therefore what thou refusest and pledge
therefore thine obedience, swearing by the said last dreadful day of judgment and by Him Who hath created all
things by His word, Whom all creatures obey. Per sedem
Baldarey et per gratiam et diligentiam tuam habuisti ab eo
hanc nalatimanamilam, as I command thee.*

CHAPTER SIXTEEN

Sex Rites

THE SEXUAL TRANCE
(AN EXAMPLE OF AN HYPNOTIC SEXUAL RITUAL)

Light two candles and place them next to a mirror. The medium shall stare into the mirror. The medium shall be passive and the operator will make passionate love to him/her. This is the medium's chance to be completely free. The operator is in charge. The medium is there simply to receive.

If you are the medium allow yourself to go deeper and deeper into ecstasy. Do not tense your body until you are ready. There is no reason to do anything until you are ready. Think a moment, feel it touch you, and let go. See the image, watch it change bit by bit and begin to feel the whirlings surround you. Now relax a bit more but not before you tense your body one last time. Be sure to tense your entire body with style. Stretch.

The operator should have performed all the necessary preliminaries. Before you go deeper ask him/her if everything is prepared for you. Once you know that the circle is made, whatever tension is left can begin to leave you. You will become the open receptacle to be filled by the spirit of your choice. Remember everything should have been agreed upon ahead of time.

Move to the bed. This is your circle of safety and joy and begin sexual stimulation.

As passion overwhelms you let it go deeper and deeper. Open up! Become empty—wider and wider—feeling nothing. Just melt.

Let everything fill you, sense the tension as it changes from pain to pleasure. Feel it build a little and then let go into it. Become bigger and bigger, let more into you. Open up—wider and wider—now. Yell, or scream if you wish or remain *as silent as you are open*.

Merge with your ecstasy. Feel no difference between yourself and what is going deeper into you. Trust completely. Drop yourself. Let the sounds of the Spirit speak.

The above sexual trance can be modified to fit your own specific needs and abilities. It is important to allow yourself to go as deep as you can. You should read the above example a couple of times before you actually start the procedure. Feel free to design and redesign your sexual trance until it suits your needs.

The use of sex and hypnosis in invocation and evocation has rarely been discussed openly. What we are doing here is dealing openly with the issue and providing a workable framework. Remember our framework is not made of stone and appropriate alterations can be made with experience.

We have found that the combination of sex and hypnosis is ideal in expanding the reception of the "medium," providing more profound and interesting data from the spirit. However, it should be pointed out that this operation should not be undertaken unless both the operator and the medium have agreed openly to undertake it and have spelt out all the details. This working requires special preparation and thus both participants should work out the details together well before they start their workings. The medium should know ahead of time that the operator will sexually exhaust the medium. This is essential for the best results. Sometimes there may be some minor discomfort for the medium in this part of the operation and the medium should allow the discomfort to dissipate at its own accord. The operator should be aware that he is manipulating high energy charges and should be very sensitive to the minor discomforts as indications that a new level of ecstasy is about to occur.

At the moment of orgasm the mind must be concentrated upon the goal of the operation, particularly in terms of visualization. This is the most difficult part of the operation, as the sex act is often distracting. In fact it is the fight between the will and the body which creates the necessary heat. Both partners should be in good health and rested and divination should be used to help select the time of the working.

A full meal should be eaten, two to three hours before the ceremony. Multiple operations for any goal are recommended. This can be on successive nights or on the same night of successive weeks.

The elixir (sperm and vaginal fluids, or sperm and sperm, or vaginal fluids and vaginal fluids, depending on gender) should be used to "give life" to a talisman or some other object (the magickal link) which is symbolic of, or connected to, the goal of the operation.

The magickal link historically is any object or substance that comes from, or has been with, the person or thing the magician desires to influence. Ideally the more intimate the object or substance the more powerful its capacity to influence the thing it is connected to.

Be specific about your goal but very general about the means by which it shall be accomplished. Do not bind or inhibit the force or spirit whose aid you request.

Be alert to dreams, omens and synchronicities, but do not look for them—you will only increase the likelihood of self delusion. Relax and enjoy.

A ritual cleansing should be performed before and after the ceremony. Rituals in the Grimoire sections can be adapted for this purpose.

In theory, the life energy (*Prana*) produced during orgasm can be directed by the Will into an "astral" or causal part of the physical world and thus influence or create events.

The most desirable situation is that both partners are equally skilled and knowledgeable regarding magickal art. If this is not possible, which is often the case, the less knowledgeable partner should be neutral in terms of the magickal visualization aspect of the ritual regardless of the role they play in the sex act. The experienced person must do the mental work.

Among the Western adaptations of Tantrik practice is one developed by Aleister Crowley which he called *Eroto-comatose lucidity* which is roughly as follows:

In this operation there can be more than two people involved. One person is selected to be the passive object of attention by the others. This person will operate as both the medium and the conduit for the force or intelligence to be conjured. This person should take care to be in good physical shape and have followed a healthy diet regimen for some time before the operation. It would also be wise to remain chaste for at least five days before the working.

The person who is the passive object will be subject to the sexual attentions of all of the other people participating; in other words, stimulated in every way possible by as many people as possible simultaneously. At this point the subject may become intoxicated with alcohol or other substances. The attentions of the other participants combined with the intoxicants should put the subject into a hypnogogic state. He or she should remain aroused but not be allowed to climax.

During this period the operating Magus should conjure the force or intelligence and ask questions of the subject regarding any visions or experiences he or she might have.

If a satisfactory response is obtained, the force is discharged to do its work and the subject allowed to climax.

The well read reader will note that some of these rituals are similar to the 9th degree procedure of one magickal Order and the 18th degree of another (both with their roots in Germany). It is important to keep in mind that both the symbolism and the techniques are significantly more ancient than either of these two groups claim.

ON WORKING WITH THE ELIXIRS

Various traditions, particularly the Hindu, ascribe real physical potency to the sexual fluids—also called the elixir.

What truth there is to this is unclear although some investigators have found remarkable effects in ancient systems of medicine.

Aleister Crowley considered the mixed male and female sexual fluids to be the literal "elixir of life." Considering his present state we may assume his faith was misplaced. However, according to one adept of his Order the reason why it didn't work for Crowley was because it wasn't made and consumed in a vacuum. Presumably future research by NASA will clarify the matter.

Be that as it may, the psycho-spiritual state of the people who produce the "elixir" may well provide it with other kinds of potencies useful in magick. One way to make use of this possible potency is to preserve and purify the substance as follows:

Take a large pot and place it on the stove. Fill the bottom of the pot with two inches of the purest drinking—ethyl—alcohol you can find. (Do not use any other type, such as rubbing—isopropyl—alcohol, as it will harm you.) Invert a small soup plate on the bottom of the pot. Place a small empty soup bowl on top of the inverted bowl.

Now place the sexual liquid in the alcohol. Invert the lid of the pot and cover it. Place ice cubes in the inverted lid and turn the heat up just enough to create steam.

The essence of the sexual fluids in their alcohol bath will now collect in the empty soup bowl. After a half an hour or so turn the heat off, collect the substance, put it in a bottle and place it in your refrigerator. From time to time you can use this "divine" substance to consecrate talismans or consume it for your health. Other uses of this material will be left up to the mind of the magician.

As this is a distillation process nothing but the purest essence of the "material" will remain. Those familiar with alchemy have understood this process for centuries allowing them to sanitize the most gross matter into the sublime.

APPENDICES
&
POSTSCRIPTS

APPENDIX I

Liber Astarte

[This article by Aleister Crowley about Bhakti Yoga is included because there is a traditional technique of Magick that in modern times has become rather obscure. This involves the communion with a spirit or demon by means of images (see illustrations) and talismans in order to absorb its qualities. This system was widely used during the Renaissance by such magicians as Mirandola and Bruno and is based on Hermetic and Classical texts. The absence of a circle in this technique is due to a different attitude toward the spirits than the Christian one. While it has a long history, it is to be used with discretion.]

0. This is the book of Uniting Himself to a particular Deity by devotion.

1. *Considerations before the Threshold.* First, concerning the choice of a particular Deity. This matter is of no import, sobeit that thou choose one suited to thine own highest nature. Howsoever, this method is not so suitable for gods austere as Saturn, or intellectual as Thoth. But for such deities as in themselves partake in anywise of love it is a perfect mode.

2. *Concerning the prime method of this Magick Art.* Let the devotee consider well that although Christ and Osiris be one, yet the former is to be worshipped with Christian, and the latter with Egyptian rites. And this although the rites themselves are ceremonially equivalent. There should, however, be *one* symbol declaring the transcending of such limitations; and with regard to the Deity also, there should

be some *one* affirmation of his identity both with all other similar gods of other nations, and with the Supreme of whom all are but partial reflections.

3. *Concerning the chief place of devotion.* This is the Heart of the devotee, and should be symbolically represented by that room or spot which he loves best. And the dearest spot therein shall be the shrine of his temple. It is most convenient if this shrine and altar should be sequestered in woods, or in a private grove, or garden. But let it be protected from the profane.

4. *Concerning the Image of the Deity.* Let there be an image of the Deity; first, because in meditation there is mindfulness induced thereby; and second, because a certain power enters and inhabits it by virtue of the ceremonies; or so it is said, and We deny it not. Let this image be the most beautiful and perfect which the devotee is able to procure; or if he be able to paint or to carve the same, it is all the better. As for Deities with whose nature no Image is compatible, let them be worshipped in an empty shrine. Such are Brahma and Allah. Also some post-captivity conceptions of Jehovah.

5. *Further concerning the shrine.* Let this shrine be furnished appropriately as to its ornaments, according to the book 777. With ivy and pine-cones, that is to say, for Bacchus, and let lay before him both grapes and wine. So also for Ceres let there be corn, and cakes; or for Diana moon-wort and pale herbs, and pure water. Further, it is well to support the shrine with talismans of the planets, signs and elements appropriate. But these should be made according to the right Ingenium of the Philosophus by the light of the book 777 during the course of his Devotion. It is also well, nevertheless, if a magick circle with the right signs and names be made beforehand.

6. *Concerning the ceremonies.* Let the Philosophus prepare a powerful Invocation of the particular Deity, according to his Ingenium. But let it consist of these several parts:

First, an Imprecation, as of a slave unto his Lord.
Second, an Oath, as of a vassal to his Liege.
Third, a Memorial, as of a child to his Parent.
Fourth, an Orison, as of a Priest unto his God.
Fifth, a Colloquy, as of a Brother with his Brother.
Sixth, a Conjuration, as of a Friend with his Friend.
Seventh, a Madrigal, as of a Lover to his Mistress.

And mark well that the first should be of awe, the second of fealty, the third of dependence, the fourth of adoration, the fifth of confidence, the sixth of comradeship, the seventh of passion.

7. *Further concerning the ceremonies.* Let then this Invocation be the principal part of an ordered ceremony. And in this ceremony let the Philosophus in no wise neglect the service of a menial. Let him sweep and garnish the place, sprinkling it with water or with wine as is appropriate to the particular Deity, and consecrating it with oil, and with such ritual as may seem him best. And let all be done with intensity and minuteness.

8. *Concerning the period of devotion, and the hours thereof.* Let a fixed period be set for the worship; and it is said that the least time is nine days by seven, and the greatest seven years by nine. And concerning the hours, let the Ceremony be performed every day thrice, or at least once, and let the sleep of the Philosophus be broken for some purpose of devotion at least once in every night.

Now to some it may seem best to appoint fixed hours for the ceremony, to others it may seem that the ceremony should be performed as the spirit moves them so to do: for this there is no rule.

9. *Concerning the Robes and Instruments.* The Wand and Cup are to be chosen for this Art; never the Sword or Dagger, never the Pantacle, unless that Pantacle chance to be of a nature harmonious. But even so it is best to keep the Wand and Cup; and if one must choose, the Cup.

For the Robes, that of a Philosophus, or that of an Adept Within is most suitable; or, the robe best fitted for the service of the particular Deity, as a bassara for Bacchus, a white robe for Vesta. So also, for Vesta, one might use for an instrument the Lamp; or the sickle, for Chronos.

10. *Concerning the Incense and Libations.* The incense should follow the nature of the particular Deity; as, mastic for Mercury, dittany for Persephone. Also the libations, as, a decoction of nightshade for Melancholia, or of Indian hemp for Uranus.

11. *Concerning the harmony of the ceremonies.* Let all these things be rightly considered, and at length, in language of the utmost beauty at the command of the Philosophus, accompanied, if he have skill, by music, and interwoven, if the particular Deity be jocund, with dancing. And all being carefully prepared and rehearsed, let it be practised daily until it be wholly rhythmical with his aspiration, and as it were, a part of his being.

12. *Concerning the variety of the ceremonies.* Now, seeing that every man differeth essentially from every other man, albeit in essence he is identical, let also these ceremonies assert their identity by their diversity. For this reason do We leave much herein to the right Ingenium of the Philosophus.

13. *Concerning the life of the devotee.* First, let his way of life be such as is pleasing to the particular Deity. Thus to invoke Neptune, let him go a-fishing; but if Hades, let him not approach the water that is hateful to Him.

14. *Further, concerning the life of the devotee.* Let him cut away from his life any act, word, or thought, that is hateful to the particular Deity; as, unchastity in the case of Artemis, evasions in the case of Ares. Besides this, he should avoid all harshness or unkindness of any kind in thought, word, or deed, seeing that above the particular Deity is One in whom all is One. Yet also he may deliberately practise cruelties, where the particular Deity manifests

His love in that manner; as in the case of Kali, and of Pan. And therefore, before the beginning of his period of devotion, let him practise according to the rules of *Liber Jugorum.*

15. *Further concerning the life of the devotee.* Now, as many are fully occupied with their affairs, let it be known that this method is adaptable to the necessities of all.

And We bear witness that this which followeth is the Crux and Quintessence of the whole Method.

First, if he have no Image, let him take anything soever, and consecrate it as an Image of his God. Likewise with his robes and instruments, his suffumigations and libations: for his Robe hath he not a night-dress; for his instrument a walking-stick; for his suffumigation a burning match, for his libation a glass of water?

But let him consecrate each thing that he useth to the service of that particular Deity, and not profane the same to any other use.

16. *Continuation.* Next, concerning his time, if it be short. Let him labour mentally upon his Invocation, concentrating it, and let him perform this Invocation in his heart whenever he hath the leisure. And let him seize eagerly upon every opportunity for this.

17. *Continuation.* Third, even if he have leisure and preparation, let him seek ever to bring inward the symbols, so that even in his well-ordered shrine the whole ceremony revolve inwardly in his heart, that is to say in the temple of his body, of which the outer temple is but an image.

For in the brain is the shrine, and there is no Image therein; and the breath of man is the incense and the libation.

18. *Continuation.* Further concerning occupation. Let the devotee transmute within the alembic of his heart every thought, or word, or act into the spiritual gold of his devotion.

As thus: eating. Let him say: "I eat this food in gratitude to my Deity that hath sent it to me, in order to gain strength for my devotion to Him."

Or: sleeping. Let him say: "I lie down to sleep, giving thanks for this blessing from my Deity, in order that I may be refreshed for new devotion to Him."

Or: reading. Let him say: "I read this book that I may study the nature of my Deity, that further knowledge of Him may inspire me with deeper devotion to Him."

Or: working. Let him say: "I drive my spade into the earth that fresh flowers (fruit, or what not) may spring up to His glory, and that I, purified by toil, may give better devotion to Him."

Or, whatever it may be that he is doing, let him reason it out in his own mind, drawing it through circumstance and circumstance to that one end and conclusion of the matter. And let him not perform the act until he hath done this.

As it is written: *Liber* VII, cap. v:

> 22. Every breath, every word, every thought, is an act of love with thee.
> 23. The beat of my heart is the pendulum of love.
> 24. The songs of me are the soft sighs:
> 25. The thoughts of me are very rapture:
> 26. And my deeds are the myriads of Thy children, the stars and the atoms.

And Remember Well, that if thou wert in truth a lover, all this wouldst thou do of thine own nature without the slightest flaw or failure in the minutest part thereof.

19. *Concerning the Lections.* Let the Philosophus read solely in his copies of the holy books of Thelema, during the whole period of his devotion. But if he weary, then let him read books which have no part whatever in love, as for recreation.

But let him copy out each verse of Thelema which bears upon this matter, and ponder them, and comment thereupon. For therein is a wisdom and a magic too deep to utter in any other wise.

20. *Concerning the Meditations.* Herein is the most potent method of attaining unto the End, for him who is thoroughly prepared, being purified by the practice of the Transmutation of deed into devotion, and consecrated by the right performance of the holy ceremonies. Yet herein is danger, for that the Mind is fluid as quicksilver, and bordereth upon the Abyss, and is beset by many sirens and devils that seduce and attack it to destroy it. Therefore let the devotee beware, and precise accurately his meditations, even as a man should build a canal from sea to sea.

21. *Continuation.* Let then the Philosophus meditate upon all love that hath ever stirred him. There is the love of David and of Jonathan, and the love of Abraham and Isaac, and the love of Lear and Cordelia, and the love of Damon and Pythias, and the love of Sappho and Atthis, and the love of Romeo and Juliet, and the love of Dante and Beatrice, and the love of Paolo and Francesca, and the love of Caesar and Lucrezia Borgia, and the love of Aucassin and Nicolette, and the love of Daphnis and Chloe, and the love of Cornelia and Caius Gracchus, and the love of Bacchus and Ariadne, and the love of Cupid and Psyche, and the love of Endymion and Artemis, and the love of Demeter and Persephone, and the love of Venus and Adonis, and the love of Lakshmi and Vishnu, and the love of Siva and Bhavani, and the love of Buddha and Ananda, and the love of Jesus and John, and many more.

Also there is the love of many saints for their particular deity, as of St Francis of Assisi for Christ, of Sri Sabhapaty Swami for Maheswara, of Abdullah Haji Shirazi for Allah, of St Ignatius Loyola for Mary, and many more.

Now do thou take one such story every night, and enact it in thy mind, grasping each identity with infinite care and zest, and do thou figure thyself as one of the lovers and thy Deity as the other. Thus do thou pass through all adventures of love, not omitting one; and to each do thou conclude: How pale a reflection is this of my love for this Deity!

Yet from each shalt thou draw some knowledge of love, some intimacy with love, that shall aid thee to perfect thy love. Thus learn the humility of love from one, its obedience from another, its intensity from a third, its purity from a fourth, its peace from yet a fifth.

So then thy love being made perfect, it shall be worthy of that perfect love of His.

22. *Further concerning meditation.* Moreover, let the Philosophus imagine to himself that he hath indeed succeeded in his devotion, and that his Lord hath appeared to him, and that they converse as may be fitting.

23. *Concerning the Mysterious Triangle.* Now then as three cords separately may be broken by a child, while those same cords duly twisted may bind a giant, let the Philosophus learn to entwine these three methods of Magic into a Spell.

To this end let him understand that as they are One, because the end is one, so are they One because the method is One, even the method of turning the mind toward the particular Deity by love in every act.

And lest thy twine slip, here is a little cord that wrappeth tightly round and round all, even the Mantram or Continuous Prayer.

24. *Concerning the Mantram or Continuous Prayer.* Let the Philosophus weave the Name of the Particular Deity into a sentence short and rhythmical; as, for Artemis: ἐπελθον, ἐπελθον, ᾽Αρτεμις or, for Shiva: Namo Shivaya namaha Aum; or, for Mary: Ave Maria; or, for Pan, χαιρε Σωτηρ κοσμον ᾽Ιω Παν ᾽Ιω Παν or, for Allah: Hua Allahu alazi lailaha illa Hua.

Let him repeat this day and night without cessation mechanically in his brain, which is thus made ready for the Advent of that Lord, and armed against all other.

25. *Concerning the Active and the Passive.* Let the Philosophus change from the active love of his particular Deity to a state of passive awaiting, even almost a repulsion, the repulsion not of distaste, but of a sublime modesty.

As it is written, *Liber LXV, ii:* 59: "I have called unto Thee, and I have journeyed unto Thee, and it availed me not." 60: "I waited patiently, and Thou wast with me from the beginning."

Then let him change back to the Active, until a veritable rhythm is established between the states, as it were the swinging of a Pendulum. But let him reflect that a vast intelligence is required for this; for he must stand as it were almost without himself to watch those phases of himself. And to do this is a high Art, and pertaineth not altogether to the grade of Philosophus. Neither is it of itself helpful, but rather the reverse, in this especial practice.

26. *Concerning Silence.* Now there may come a time in the course of this practice when the outward symbols of devotion cease, when the soul is as it were dumb in the presence of its God. Mark that this is not a cessation, but a transmutation of the barren seed of prayer into the green shoot of yearning. This yearning is spontaneous, and it shall be left to grow, whether it be sweet or bitter. For often times it is as the torment of hell in which the soul burns and writhes unceasingly. Yet it ends, and at its end continue openly thy Method.

27. *Concerning Dryness.* Another state wherein at times the soul may fall is this dark night. And this is indeed purifying in such depths that the soul cannot fathom it. It is less like pain than like death. But it is the necessary death that comes before the rising of a body glorified.

This state must be endured with fortitude; and no means of alleviating it may be employed. It may be broken up by the breaking up of the whole Method, and a return to the world without. This cowardice not only destroys the value of all that has gone before, but destroys the value of the

Oath of Fealty that thou hast sworn, and makes thy Will a mockery to men and gods.

28. *Concerning the Deceptions of the Devil.* Note well that in this state of dryness a thousand seductions will lure thee away; also a thousand means of breaking thine oath in spirit without breaking it in letter. Against this thou mayst repeat the words of thine oath aloud again and again until the temptation be overcome.

Also the devil will represent to thee that it were much better for this operation that thou do thus and thus, and seek to affright thee by fears for thy health or thy reason.

Or he may send against thee visions worse than madness.

Against all this there is but one remedy, the Discipline of thine Oath. So then thou shalt go through ceremonies meaningless and hideous to thee, and blaspheme shalt thou against thy Deity and curse Him. And this mattereth little, for it is not thou, so be that thou adhere to the Letter of thine Obligation. For thy Spiritual Sight is closed, and to trust it is to be led unto the precipice, and hurled therefrom.

29. *Further of this matter.* Now also subtler than all these terrors are the Illusions of Success. For one instant's self-satisfaction or Expansion of thy Spirit, especially in this state of dryness, and thou art lost. For thou mayst attain the False Union with the Demon himself. Beware also of even the pride which rises from having resisted the temptations.

But so many and so subtle are the wiles of Choronzon that the whole world could not contain their enumeration.

The answer to one and all is the persistence in the literal fulfillment of the routine. Beware, then, last, of that devil who shall whisper in thine ear that the letter killeth, but the spirit giveth life, and answer: Except a corn of wheat fall into the ground and die, it abideth alone; but if it die, it bringeth forth much fruit.

Yet shalt thou also beware of disputation with the devil, and pride in the cleverness of thine answers to him. Therefore, if thou hast not lost the power of silence, let it be first and last employed against him.

30. *Concerning the Enflaming of the Heart.* Now learn that thy methods are dry one and all. Intellectual exercises, moral exercises, they are not Love. Yet as a man, rubbing two dry sticks together for long, suddenly found a spark, so also from time to time will true love leap unasked into thy meditation. Yet this shall die and be reborn again and again. It may be that thou hast no tinder near.

In the end shall come suddenly a great flame and a devouring, and burn thee utterly.

Now of these sparks, and of these splutterings of flame, and of these beginnings of the Infinite Fire, thou shalt thus be aware. For the sparks thy heart shall leap up, and thy ceremony or meditation or toil shall seem of a sudden to go of its own will; and for the little flames this shall be increased in volume and intensity; and for the beginnings of the Infinite Fire thy ceremony shall be caught up unto ravishing song, and thy meditation shall ecstasy, and thy toil shall be a delight exceeding all pleasure thou hast ever known.

And of the Great Flame that answereth thee it may not be spoken; for therein is the End of this Magick Art Devotion.

31. *Considerations with regard to the use of symbols.* It to be noted that persons of powerful imagination, will and intelligence have no need of these material symbols. There have been certain saints who are capable of love for an idea as such without it being otherwise than deaded by *idolising* it, to use this word in its true sense. Thus one may be impassioned of beauty, without even the need of so small a concretion of it as "the beauty of Apollo," "the beauty of roses," "the beauty of Attis." Such persons are rare; it may be doubted whether Plato himself attained to any vision of absolute beauty without attaching to it material objects in the first place. A second class is able to contemplate ideals through this veil; a third class need a double veil, and

cannot think of the beauty of a rose without a rose before them. For such is Method of most use; yet let them know that there is this danger therein, that they may mistake the gross body the symbol for the idea made concrete thereby.

32. *Considerations of further danger to those not purged material thought.* Let it be remembered that in the nature the love itself is danger. The lust of the satyr for the nymph is indeed of the same nature as the affinity of quicklime for water on the one hand, and of the love of Ab for Ama on the other; so also is the triad Osiris, Isis, Horus like that of a horse, mare, foal, and of red, blue, purple. And this is the foundation of Correspondences.

But it were false to say, "Horus is a foal" or, "Horus is purple." One may say, "Horus resembles a foal in this respect, that he is the offspring of two complementary beings."

33. *Further of this matter. So* also many have said truly that all is one, and falsely that since earth is That One, and ocean is That One, therefore earth is ocean. Unto Him good is illusion, and evil is illusion; therefore good is evil. By this fallacy of logic are many men destroyed.

Moreover, there are those who take the image for the God; as who should say, my heart is in Tiphereth, and an Adeptus is in Tiphereth; I am therefore an adept.

And in this practice the worst danger is this, that the love which is its weapon should fail in one of two ways.

First, if the love lack any quality of love, so long is it not ideal love. For it is written of the Perfected One: "There is no member of my body which is not the member of some god." Therefore let not the Philosophus despise any form of love, but harmonize all. As it is written, *Liber LXI, 32:* "So therefore Perfection abideth not in the Pinnacles or in the Foundation, but in the harmony of One with all."

Second, if any part of this love exceed, there is disease therein. As, in the love of Othello for Desdemona, love's jealousy overcame love's tenderness, so may it be in this love of a particular Deity. And this is more likely, since in this divine love no element may be omitted.

It is by virtue of this completeness that no human love may in any way attain to more than to foreshadow a little part thereof.

34. *Concerning Mortifications.* These are not necessary to this method. On the contrary, they may destroy the concentration, as counter-irritants to, and so alleviations of, the supreme mortification which is the Absence of the Deity invoked.

Yet as in mortal love arises a distaste for food, or a pleasure in things naturally painful, this perversion should be endured and allowed to take its course. Yet not to the interference with natural bodily health, whereby the instrument of the soul might be impaired.

And concerning sacrifices for love's sake, they are natural to this Method, and right.

But concerning voluntary privations and tortures, without use save as against the devotee, they are generally not natural to healthy natures, and wrong. For they are selfish. To scourge one's self serves not one's master; yet to deny one's self bread that one's child may have cake, the act of a true mother.

35. *Further concerning Mortifications.* If thy body, on which thou ridest, be so disobedient a beast that by no means will he travel in the desired direction, or if thy mind be baulkish and eloquent as Balaam's fabled Ass, then let the practice be abandoned. Let the shrine be covered in sackcloth, and do thou put on habits of lamentation, and abide alone. And do thou return most austerely to the practice of *Liber Jugorum,* testing thyself by a standard higher than that hitherto accomplished, and punishing effractions with a heavier goad. Nor do thou return to thy devotion until that body and mind are tamed and trained to all manner of peaceable going.

36. *Concerning minor methods adjuvant in the cere-monies. I. Rising on the planes.* By this method mayst thou assist the imagination at the time of concluding thine Invo-cation. Act as taught in *Liber 0,* by the light of *Liber 777.*

37. *Concerning minor methods adjuvant in the cere-monies. II. Talismanic magic.* Having made by thine Inge-nium a talisman or pantacle to represent the particular Deity, and consecrated it with infinite love and care, do thou burn it ceremonially before the shrine, as if thereby giving up the shadow for the substance. But it is useless to do this unless thou do really in thine heart value the talis-man beyond all else that thou hast.

38 *Concerning minor methods adjuvant in the cere-monies. III. Rehearsal.* It may assist if the traditional histo-ry of the particular Deity be rehearsed before him; perhaps this is best done in dramatic form. This method is the main one recommended in the *Exercitios Espirituales* of St Ignatius, whose work may be taken as a model. Let the Philosophus work out the legend of his own particular Deity, and apportioning days to events, live that life in imagination, exercising the five senses in turn, as occasion arises.

39. *Concerning minor matters adjuvant in the cere-monies. IV. Duresse.* This method consists in cursing a deity recalcitrant; as, threatening ceremonially "to burn the blood of Osiris, and to grind down his bones to powder." This method is altogether contrary to the spirit of love, unless the particular Deity be himself savage and relentless; as, Jehovah or Kali. In such a case the desire to perform constraint and cursing may be the sign of the assimilation of the spirit of the devotee with that of his God, and so an advance to the Union with Him.

40. *Concerning the value of this particular form of Union or Samadhi.* All Samadhi is defined as the ecstatic union of subject and object in consciousness, with the result that a

third thing arises which partakes in no way of the nature of the two.

It would seem at first sight that it is of no importance whatever to choose an object of meditation. For example, the Samadhi called Atmadarshana might arise from simple concentration of the thought on an imagined triangle, or on the heart.

But as the union of two bodies in chemistry may be endothermic or exothermic, the combination of Oxygen with Nitrogen is gentle, while that of Oxygen with Hydrogen is explosive; and as it is found that the most heat is disengaged as a rule by the union of bodies most opposite in character, and that the compound resulting from such is most stable, so it seems reasonable to suggest that the most important and enduring Samadhi results from the contemplation of the Object most opposite to the devotee. On other planes, it has been suggested that the most opposed types make the best marriages and produce the healthiest children. The greatest pictures and operas are those in which violent extremes are blended, and so generally in every field of activity. Even in mathematics, the greatest parallelogram is formed if the lines composing it are set at right angles.

41. *Conclusions from the foregoing.* It may then be suggested to the Philosophus, that although his work will be harder his reward will be greater if he choose a Deity most remote from his own nature. This method is harder and higher than that of *Liber E.* For a simple object as there suggested is of the same nature as the commonest things of life, while even the meanest Deity is beyond uninitiated human understanding. On the same plane, too, Venus is nearer to man than Aphrodite, Aphrodite than Isis, Isis than Babalon, Babalon than Nuit.

Let him decide therefore according to his discretion on the one hand and his aspiration on the other: and let not one outrun his fellow.

42. *Further concerning the value of this Method.* Certain objections arise. Firstly, in the nature of all human love is illusion, and a certain blindness. Nor is there any true love below the Veil of the Abyss. For this reason We give this Method to the Philosophus, as the reflection of the Exempt Adept, who reflects the Magister Templi and the Magus. Let then the Philosophus attain this method as a foundation of the higher Methods to be given to him when he attains those higher grades.

Another objection lies in the partiality of this Method. This is equally a defect characteristic of the Grade.

43. *Concerning a notable danger of Success.* It may occur that owing to the tremendous power of the Samadhi, over-coming all other memories as it should and does do, that the mind of the devotee may be obsessed, so that he declare his particular Deity to be sole God and Lord. This error has been the foundation of all dogmatic religions, and so the cause of more misery than all other errors combined.

The Philosophus is peculiarly liable to this because from the nature of the Method he cannot remain sceptical; he must for the time believe in his particular Deity. But let him *(1)* consider that this belief is only a weapon in his hands, *(2)* affirm sufficiently that his Deity is but an emanation or reflection or eidolon of a Being beyond him, as was said in Paragraph 2. For if he fail herein, since man cannot remain permanently in Samadhi, the memorized Image in his mind will be degraded, and replaced by the corresponding Demon, to his utter ruin.

Therefore, after Success, let him not delight overmuch in his Deity, but rather busy himself with his other work, not permitting that which is but a step to become a goal. As it is written also, *Liber CLXXXV:* "remembering that Philoso-phy is the Equilibrium of him that is in the House of Love."

44. *Concerning secrecy, and the rites of Blood.* During this practice it is most wise that the Philosophus utter no word concerning his working, as if it were a Forbidden

Love that consumeth him. But let him answer fools according to their folly; for since he cannot conceal his love from his fellows, he must speak to them as they may understand.

And as many Deities demand sacrifices, one of men, another of cattle, a third of doves, let these sacrifices be replaced by the true sacrifices in thine own heart. Yet if thou must symbolise them outwardly for the hardness of thine heart, let thine own blood, and not another's, be It before that altar.

Nevertheless, forget not that this practice is dangerous, and may cause the manifestation of evil things, hostile and malicious, to thy great hurt.

45. *Concerning a further sacrifice.* Of this it shall be understood that nothing is to be spoken; nor need anything be spoken to him that hath wisdom to comprehend the number of the paragraph. And this sacrifice is fatal beyond all, unless it be a *sacrificium* indeed. Yet there those who have dared and achieved thereby.

46. *Concerning yet a further sacrifice.* Here it is spoken actual mutilation. Such acts are abominable; and while they may bring success in this Method, form an absolute bar to all further progress.

And they are in any case more likely to lead to madness then to Samadhi. He indeed who purposeth them is already mad.

47. *Concerning human affection.* During this practice thou shalt in no wise withdraw thyself from human relations, only figuring to thyself that thy father or thy brother or thy wife is as it were an image of thy particular Deity. Thus shall they gain, and not lose, by thy working. Only in the case of thy wife this is difficult, since she is more to thee than all others, and in this case thou mayst: with temperance, lest her personality overcome and destroy that of thy Deity.

48. *Concerning the Holy Guardian Angel.* Do thou in no wise confuse this invocation with that.

49. *The Benediction.* And so may the Love that passeth all Understanding keep your hearts and minds through IAΩ AΔΩNAI XABAΩ and through Babalon of the City of the Pyramids, and through Astarte the Starry One green-girdled in the name Ararita.

Amen.

APPENDIX II

Planetary Attributes

PLANETS & THE DAYS OF THE WEEK

Monday	Moon
Tuesday	Mars
Wednesday	Mercury
Thursday	Jupiter
Friday	Venus
Saturday	Saturn
Sunday	Sun

PLANETARY NATURES

Saturn:

In the days and hours of Saturn you can conjure the souls of the dead, conjure familiar spirits to bring you oracles in dreams, to cause good or evil luck, for business, goods, enterprises, to acquire learning or information, and for operations of death, hatred and discord.

Jupiter:

In the days and hours of Jupiter you can obtain honors, acquire money, gain friendship and patrons, improve health, and acquire general good fortune.

Mars:

In the days and hours of Mars are good for all activities regarding war, to obtain military honors and rank, to acquire courage, to destroy enemies, to cause ruin, slaughter, cruelty, discord and to wound and give death.

Sun:

In the days and hours of the Sun are good for obtaining temporal wealth, hope, gain, fortune, for telling of the future, obtaining the aid of princes to eliminate hostility, and to make friends.

Venus:

In the days and hours of Venus are good for friendships, kindness, love, erotic endeavors, and for traveling.

Mercury:

In the days and hours of Mercury, are good for eloquence, and intelligence, skill in business, science, divination and to discover hidden enemies and deceit and those guilty of theft.

Moon:

In the days and hours of the Moon are good for voyages, messages, navigation, reconciliation and all activities having to do with water.

TABLE OF PLANETARY HOURS

(The first hour of the day is midnight until one o'clock. After the cycle of twelve is completed, it repeats until the next midnight.)

	SUNDAY	MONDAY	TUESDAY	WEDNESDAY
1.	Sun	Moon	Mars	Mercury
2.	Venus	Saturn	Sun	Moon
3.	Mercury	Jupiter	Venus	Saturn
4.	Moon	Mars	Mercury	Jupiter
5.	Saturn	Sun	Moon	Mars
6.	Jupiter	Venus	Saturn	Sun
7.	Mars	Mercury	Jupiter	Venus
8.	Sun	Moon	Mars	Mercury
9.	Venus	Saturn	Sun	Moon
10.	Mercury	Jupiter	Venus	Saturn
11.	Moon	Mars	Mercury	Jupiter

12. Saturn	Sun	Moon	Mars

THURSDAY	FRIDAY	SATURDAY
1. Jupiter	Venus	Saturn
2. Mars	Mercury	Jupiter
3. Sun	Moon	Mars
4. Venus	Saturn	Sun
5. Mercury	Jupiter	Venus
6. Moon	Mars	Mercury
7. Saturn	Sun	Moon
8. Jupiter	Venus	Saturn
9. Mars	Mercury	Jupiter
10. Sun	Moon	Mars
11. Venus	Saturn	Sun
12. Mercury	Jupiter	Venus

From 12:00 Noon To 12:00 Midnight

SUNDAY	MONDAY	TUESDAY	WEDNESDAY
13. Sun	Moon	Mars	Mercury
14. Venus	Saturn	Sun	Moon
15. Mercury	Jupiter	Venus	Saturn
16. Moon	Mars	Mercury	Jupiter
17. Saturn	Sun	Moon	Mars
18. Jupiter	Venus	Saturn	Sun
19. Mars	Mercury	Jupiter	Venus
20. Sun	Moon	Mars	Mercury
21. Venus	Saturn	Sun	Moon
22. Mercury	Jupiter	Venus	Saturn
23. Moon	Mars	Mercury	Jupiter
24. Saturn	Sun	Moon	Mars

THURSDAY	FRIDAY	SATURDAY
13. Jupiter	Venus	Saturn
14. Mars	Mercury	Jupiter
15. Sun	Moon	Mars
16. Venus	Saturn	Sun
17. Mercury	Jupiter	Venus
18. Moon	Mars	Mercury
19. Saturn	Sun	Moon
20. Jupiter	Venus	Saturn
21. Mars	Mercury	Jupiter
22. Sun	Moon	Mars
23. Venus	Saturn	Sun
24. Mercury	Jupiter	Venus

PLANETARY COLORS & METALS

Monday	Moon	Silver	Silver
Tuesday	Mars	Red	Iron
Wednesday	Mercury	Orange	Mercury
Thursday	Jupiter	Blue	Tin
Friday	Venus	Green	Copper
Saturday	Saturn	Black	Lead
Sunday	Sun	Yellow	Gold

FUMES & PLANETS

Moon	Jasmine
Mars	Tobacco or Benzoin
Mercury	Storax or Mastic or Mace
Jupiter	Cedar or Saffron
Venus	Rose or Sandalwood or Myrtle
Saturn	Asafoetida or Sulfur
Sun	Olibanum or Cinnamon

PLANETARY DEMONS & INTELLIGENCE
WITH SEALS & SIGILS

PLANET	DEMON	INTELLIGENCE
Moon	Chasahmodai	Malcah Betarshisim
Mars	Bartzabel	Graphiel
Mercury	Taphthartharath	Tiriel
Jupiter	Hismael	Yophiel

PLANET	DEMON	INTELLIGENCE
Venus	Kedemel	Hagiel
Saturn	Zazel	Agiel
Sun	Sorath	Nakhiel

APPENDIX III

Sample Pact

I—[name] on this [day] of [month] in the year [year] formally ally myself with the spirit [Name] and his servants for our mutual benefit in order that I may achieve the following goals: [Note: the goals are the most important part of the pact and should be well thought out. The goals can be highly personal as no one need ever see this document.]

In return for the above benefits I will deliver to the spirits the following offerings and services: (Note: list all the offerings previously determined by divination or intuition. Be very specific and do not promise something you do not intend to give.)

I charge the spirit that by agreeing to this document he binds himself and makes himself subject to punishment if he should disregard his part of this agreement or bring harm to me or mine.

[Note: the pact can dissolved upon completion of the agreement or if the operator is honestly dissatisfied with the demon.]

[Signed in your own blood.]

[On the side opposite your signature, draw the sigil or picture of the demon.]

[Note: sterile lancets are easily available at most drug stores.]

APPENDIX IV

Fragment Of A German Faust Manuscript

Introduction to the Faust Manuscript
(Companion to Chapter Six: The Legacy of Faust)

The following is a system of evocation for seven planetary demons from a book that, at a guess, dates from seventeenth century Germany. It is probably from one of the numerous *"Harrowings of Hell"* attributed to Faust produced between the early seventeenth to the early nineteenth centuries.

We discovered it as an end fragment of a book of charms attributed to Moses (!) and only realized what it was when we saw the telltale name of Mephistophilis (and Prospero's Ariel!). It is included here as a short, coherent piece which can be adapted for use with other systems in the book, especially the much more lengthy *Honorees*.

The book had no imprint date, company name, or copyright and was printed on the cheapest kind of newsprint. It was found in a flea market.

The late professor E.M. Butler (in *Ritual Magic*) has whimsically suggested that the seven Faustian demons are survivals of the seven Maskim of the Akkadians. Certainly they are related to the planetary demons of the Cabbalists.

For the practitioner's information:

AZIEL is related to the earth and sea.

ARIEL commands lost treasures.

MARUBEL assists in obtaining secret knowledge.

MEPHISTOPHILIS, of course, is king of familiar spirits and can supply the magician with other familiar spirits.

BARUBEL is a master of all arts, and can presumably teach same.

AZIABEL is yet another treasure spirit, especially of mountains.

ANITUEL is compared to the serpent of paradise, and confers great honors.

The magus is urged to select an appropriate time and day to begin (using, presumably a table of planetary hours) and to continue his evocations for an extended period of days.

Good luck.

EVOCATION FOR THE MAGICAL CIRCLE.
TO BE PLACED OR DRAWN ON THE GROUND.

Ego (name) consercro et benedico istum Circulum per Nomina Dei Attissimi in ec Scripta, ut sit mihi et omnibus Scutum at Protectio Dei Fortissimi Elohim Invincibilie contra omnes malignos Spiritus gerurmque Potestates. In Nomine Dei Patris Dei Filii Dei Spiritus Sancti. Amen.

Upon your entrance into this Circle speak as follows:

Tetragrammaton, Theos, Ischiros, Athanatos, Messias, Imas, Kyrie, Eleison. Amen.

After you have entered the Circle begin your operation with the following prayer from *Psalm 91:*

He that dwelleth in the secret place of the Most High shall abide under the shadow of the Almighty.

I will say of the LORD, He is my refuge and my fortress: my God; in him will I trust.

Surely he shall deliver thee from the snare of the fowler, and from the noisome pestilence.

He shall cover thee with his feathers, and under his wings shalt thou trust: his truth shall be thy shield and buckler.

Thou shalt not be afraid for the terror by night; nor for the arrow that flieth by day;

Nor for the pestilence that walketh in darkness; nor for the destruction that wasteth at noonday.

Because thou hast made the LORD, which is my refuge, even the most High, thy habitation;

There shall no evil befall thee, neither shall any plague come nigh thy dwelling.

For he shall give his angels charge over thee, to keep thee in all thy ways.

Because he hath set his love upon me, therefore will I deliver him: I will set him on high, because he hath known my name.

He shall call upon me, and I will answer him: I will be with him in trouble; I will deliver him, and honour him.

With long life will I satisfy him, and show him my salvation.

Even so help me and all them that seek thy holy God the Father, God the Son, God the Holy Ghost. Amen.

Evocation Of Azielis

Agla Cadelo, Sambe, Caclem, Awenhatoacoro, Aziel, Zorwotho, Yzewoth, Xoro, Quotwe, Theosy, Meweth, Xosoy, Yachyros, Gaba, Hagay, Staworo, Wyhaty, Ruoso Xuatho, Rum, Rowoth, Zyros, Quaylos, Wewer, Vegath, Wysor, Wuzoy, Noses, Aziel.

Evocation Of Arielis

Yschyros, Teor Zebaoth, Wyzeth, Yzathos, Xyro, Xywethorowoy, Xantho, Wiros, Rurawey, Ymowe, Noswathosway, Wuvnethowesy, Zebaoth, Yvmo, Zvswethonowe, Yschyrioskay, Ulathos, Wyzoy, Yrsawe, Xyzeth, Durobijthaos Wuzowethus, Yzweoy, Zaday, Zywaye, Hagathorowos, Yachyros, Imas, Tetragrammaton, Ariel.

Evocation Of Marubelis

Adonay, Jehova, Zebaoth, Theos, Yzhathoroswe, Wehox-ymathos, Zosim, Yghoroy, Vegorym, Abaij, Wogos, Gijghijm, Zewoij, Ykosowe, Wethym, Kijzwe, Uijwoth, Omegros, Hehgewe, Zebaoij, Wezator, Zibuo, Sijbetho, Ythos, Zeatijm, Wovoe, Sijwoijmwethij, Pharvij, Zwor, Wefgos, Ruhen Hvbathoroos, Stawows, Zfijen, Zijwowij, Haros, Worse, Yswet, Zebaoth, Agia, Marbuel.

Evocation Of Mephistophilis

Messias, Adonaij, Wforus, Xathor, Yxewe, Sorawijs, Yxaron, Wegharh, Zljhalor, Weghaij, Wesoron, Xoxijwe, Zijwohwawetho, Ragthoswatho, Zebaoth, Adonaij, Zijwetho Aglaij, Wijzathe, Zadaij, Zijebo Xosthoy, Athlato, Zsewey, Zyxyzet, Ysche, Sarsewu, Zyzyrn, Deworonhathbo, Xyxewe, Syzwe, Theos, Yschaos Woronbefgosy, Gefgowe, Hegor, Quaratho, Zywe, Messias, Abarabi, Mephistophilis.

Evocation Of Barbuelis

Yschiros, Imns, Zebaoth, Otheos, Kumethosorym, Zylo-
hym, Zaday, Yschowe, Quyos, Zenhatorowav, Yzwesor,
Xywoy, Yzyryr, Zalijmo, Zabaoth, Adonaii, Messios,
Aglaabaij, Stoweos, Hijwethos, Ycoros, Zijwetho, Uwoim,
Chamoweo, Zijzobeth, Sotho, Emnohalj, Zedije, Huwethos,
Chorij, Yzquoos, Lijraije, Weghoijm, Xiixor, Waijos,
Gofaljme, Toroswe, Yeijros, Emanuel, Imas, Barbuel.

Evocation Of Aziabelis

Thoeos, Ygweto, Yzgowoij, Quiseo, Wijzope, Xorsoij,
Nowetho, Yxose, Haguthou, Xoro, Theos, Magowo, Wijzo-
sorwothe, Xaroshaij, Zebaoth, Emanuel, Messia, Yzijwo-
tho, Zadaaij, Xexhatosijmeij, Buwatho, Ywewet, Xijrathor,
Zijbos, Malhaton, Yzos, Uzewor, Raguil, Wewot, Yzwewe,
Quorhijm, Zadob, Zibathor, Weget, Zijzawe, Ulijzor,
Tretragaammaton, Aziabel.

Evocation Of Aniquelis

Thoeos, Aba, Aaba, Aba, Agathoswaij, Yzoroij, Ywetho, Quardos, Quasoai Uschjjros, Cijmoe, Qowathim, Gefoij, Zarobe, Weghatj, Ohegathorowaij, Mesows, Xalose, Waghthorsowe, Wephatho, Yzebo, Stotilwethonaij, Quorathon, Sijbo, Mephor, Wijhose, Zaloros, Ruetho, Zebaathonaijwos, Zijweth, Ycarij, Ruwethonowe, Ruiathosowaij, Zebaoth, Messias, Aiquel.

POSTSCRIPT

War In Heaven

As I (S.J. Black) write this, the book is nearly ready to go to press and while it has largely come out as it was envisioned, I felt that something personal had to be added at the end, that something was missing, or had to be clarified.

This book originally grew out of a casual remark that I made to Dr. Hyatt some time ago, that there were no really good editions of the three Grimoires in Part II. I was thinking in terms of something really usable in the way that the Key of Solomon is usable, but the book grew into something else, backasswards as it were, until it became what you now hold.

It is now two months since the Walpurgis Nacht when Los Angeles transmogrified itself into a little vision of Hell after four members of the LAPD were found innocent on all counts by an all white jury for crimes of violence that literally the entire world saw them commit. It is now almost a year since Randall Terry, the leader of the ironically named "Operation Rescue" had his reactionary troops terrorize the young women of Wichita, Kansas, and declare the nation in a state of cultural civil war.

He is correct. We have been in this war for some decades, and it will proceed apace—sometimes visible, sometimes not—long after we are dead. This "war" is the dissonance between an obsolete, sick and dying world-view and the new one that is not fully formed.

Yet, dying though it may be, the senile old world, as the Mage Dr. Israel Regardie often said, still holds us in its grip in many ways; and the purpose of this book came to be twofold: partly a statement of principles, and partly to present a tool for self-liberation and empowerment, a tool generally neglected and deeply feared.

I can best illustrate the reasons for our particular choices with some personal vignettes:

I have a close friend (I hope he won't murder me for telling this story) who is an Episcopal priest. He also makes his living as a bartender. (I have often suspected that one is good practice for the other.) He is extremely well-read, and has been so since he was a small child. One day—how the conversation began, I don't recall—we were talking about religion and I said, "You realize of course that almost the entire Jesus myth was taken from the story of the Sun God Mithras." To my surprise he responded, "Of course. I know history." I was pleasantly surprised by this, since most seminary-trained people with whom I have had similar discussions possessed a remarkable hole (or memory failure) in their education when it came to early Christianity and its Roman/Hellenic sources.

After a while, though, it bothered me a little and I asked, "Have you ever told your parishioners—in a class or sermon—that the New Testament is taken from Pagan sources?"

This bothered him. His mouth tightened and he said, "No."

I thought this was very strange. By no means did he make even a significant percentage of his living as a priest, and by his own admission didn't believe the Bible was a historical document, and yet, he wouldn't educate his congregation and he didn't quit. I was so struck by this lapse of consistency—so totally out of character—that I would sometimes torment him in public by saying (in a very loud voice), "Have you told your congregation the truth about Jesus yet?"

His squirming usually lifted my spirits.

But of course, it really isn't a joke.

The last time I pulled this stunt I was in a slightly meaner mood. He was talking some Biblical rubbish with someone, and I said, "Tell him about Mithras." The man he was speaking to looked puzzled and he looked embarrassed. Then (going, perhaps, a bit too far) I asked, "Aren't you ever ashamed to be pushing something that hurts so many people and that you know to be untrue?"

He crossed his arms and looked away in annoyance.

But he didn't say "no."

I have another friend, an acquaintance really, who is a gay man in his mid-forties. He works at one of the largest newspapers in the country. He is also a morbidly devout graduate of the largest Protestant seminary in the Midwest and is masochistically fond of expounding the virtues of obedience to "god." So I asked him, as I ask everyone who presents this "paradox" to me, "How do you justify being gay and Christian?"

His response, to my utter astonishment, was that he didn't see it as an issue. I pointed out to him the direct and violent condemnations of homosexuality both in the Bible and by the church in which he was trained. As I recall, I referred to the condemnation of "sodomites" and pointed out that he *was* one. He told me that "sodomite" didn't really refer to homosexuals (!) but meant, instead, "dissolute, immoral people." I invited him to check into the matter in any dictionary—and diplomatically refrained from pointing out his fondness for male prostitutes.

I have had my apartment broken into and my belongings searched by Christian neighbors who discovered I wasn't "one of them." (And oh, what a story I have to tell about *that*.) Presumably they were searching for a stockpile of sacrificed babies. Their aim was not theft and not once did it occur to them that they were committing a crime.

I have spoken to black men so desperate to be white that they put on the costume of right-wing republicanism.

I have watched the once-promising "neo-pagan" movement degenerate into a gaggle of social outcasts who spend their time spouting moralisms and dressing like refugees from *Dungeons and Dragons*.

And sadly, I have seen the various organizations who claim to follow Aleister Crowley fade into religious fadism, and are more worried about whether or not Crowley is accepted as the "World Teacher" by academics than the serious practice of the magic arts.

My point? The *basic pattern* of religious thought in our culture holds us in a grip which the common man will do anything to maintain, no matter how destructive to himself or others. This is involuntary and unconscious. Christianity, in all its forms, tends toward mental illness—and depends on it to survive. All religion in this culture, whatever it *claims* to be, will tend to imitate Christianity unless the program is broken. And it is the purpose of the "black arts" of the Eastern and Western traditions to break that program, that grip. They do not ignore, they confront, which is why they are considered evil.

That people are trapped by the world they live in is no one's fault. That many people hold the cell door closed themselves still confuses me despite my experience.

The mass of men, Christian homosexuals, black Republicans and Jewish Nazis, all who through laziness or inability conspire with Church and State to do themselves harm, are no better than slaves. If they choose to live their lives with shackles on, so be it.

For those few of you who have the courage to give your enemies a name and fight them (even though you may not win) however deep inside they may be, we have tried to show that the path is still where it always was—right at the heart of what you have been taught to fear the most.

Sebastian Jason Black
Los Angeles, July 1992

POST POSTSCRIPT

You Get What You Ask For

In a different vein, I (C.S. Hyatt) vacationed on an island "paradise." Arriving exhausted I felt ready for bed but was kept awake by a great sense of foreboding. The next morning I awoke late and had a breakfast which included four scotches. I still sensed a terrible feeling coming from the place. I called my travel agent and she informed me that since I had prepaid the trip I was stuck there for two weeks unless I could get a note from a Doctor saying I was sick. She added that the illness couldn't be preexisting. Except for claiming mental illness I felt hopeless for an excuse that would pass the medical examiner. So I bit the bullet and tried to enjoy myself. I thought a good workout might help so I went to the gym. But before I did I asked Lucifuge to act in my behalf offering him a proper trade. However, I warned him that the "sign" had to be physical and not psychological. I left for the gym, exercised for twenty minutes or so and walked back to my room. On the way I brushed up against a bush which was sticking out a foot or so on the pathway. I felt a sting under my right breast and a horrible burning sensation. I thought little of it except that I had been stung. I looked at the wound put some medication on it and took a nap. I later awoke, went to dinner, watched some TV and went to sleep.

The next morning the bite had swollen a little but I had expected that. So I started my day with breakfast, walked a mile or two, swam for a few hours and rested. It was late in the afternoon so it was my "tea time." I went to one bar which was closed so I went to the pool bar and had a drink. While waiting for my second drink I heard a scream and saw the bartender running out of the bar. She was crying and pounding the wall. Being used to craziness I thought little of it as I began to scratch my breast more vigorously. Wanting a second drink more desperately now I flagged down the second bartender who was yelling at the first bartender to go home and cool down. I got my drink sometime later and asked the bartender what was wrong with his associate. He replied that their "best" friend had just drowned. I felt a sense of mild shock finished my drink and went to my room to change for dinner.

I had a wonderful dinner except for the scratching and burning of my right breast. I finished my meal went to my room took off my shirt and my breast had expanded sideways by four inches. It was swollen and multi-colored. Needless to say I became concerned. It was 9:00 PM so I called the front desk for help. The operator said it was probably a mosquito bite. I told her that if it was it must have been a foot or so long. She called the doctor who called me back by 9:30. I told him my symptoms and he said that he would be right over. He arrived, looked at my bite and said that he had only seen four such reactions in all of his years of practice. He put me on antibiotics and other drugs and told me to call him in the morning.

I awoke at 8:00 AM and looked at my breast. I called him immediately. My breast had swollen another 2 inches. The little bite had now grown to a 6 inch circle. He told me that I might require intravenous antibiotics but first I should try some other type orally. I told him I had an allergy to one of its cousins. He became concerned and so did I. I told him that I would rather take my chances in Los Angeles where I had my own doctor and complete insurance coverage. I told him that I would need a letter so I could get my money back. He agreed immediately on the proviso that I continue taking two safer, but less effective, types of antibiotics until

I saw my doctor. I quickly agreed, took a cab to his office, picked up the note and the pills.

Now I had the precious note but no plane reservations. I checked out of the hotel and then called the airlines. There were seats available on the next flight out but I couldn't make it in time unless the "Gods" were with me. I hired a speed boat which rushed me to the main Island at 30 knots. I had a cab waiting which got me to the airport with over 40 minutes to spare.

I arrived in Los Angeles late at night and had an appointment with my own doctor the next morning. My breast began to get smaller, although it was greatly discolored and swollen. He drew blood and gave me more antibiotics and pain pills. He said the weekend would be when I would know whether hospitalization for intravenous antibiotics and surgery would be necessary to remove pus pockets. Monday I went back to his office. The swelling was gone. All that was left was some minor discoloration and the puncture wound.

Apparently I got my physical manifestation. It is interesting to note in passing that the bushes where the beast that struck me lay were trimmed the morning after my bite. If I was one day late I would have never brushed up against them. The spider or "magical" beast would have had to find another way to work his will.

I leave it to the reader to explain this away.

Christopher S. Hyatt, Ph.D.
Los Angeles
July, 1992

AFTERWORD TO
THE SECOND EDITION

This book first appeared prior to our now infamous crossing of the Pacific in the Spring of 1993. The book met with the usual criticism from the Occult community, commenting on its dangers particularly for novices in search of power and money. With this, of course, we agree—but not on moral grounds. We, as seasoned practitioners, have experienced the "fall out" of any intense magical operation. In some cases we got what we were after along with an array of unpleasant "accidents." Some of these accidents were more than unpleasant and this is probably due to the nature of all spirits who operate by a different set of rules than we humans.

Others, in their usual stupidity, attacked the OTO (Ordo Templi Orientis), claiming that this book was sponsored by the Order. This book is neither sponsored by the OTO nor is it sanctioned by the Order. It is true that Mr. Black and Dr. Hyatt are members of the OTO but this in no way "proves" that the OTO had anything to do with this work.

Other criticisms took the form of threats from the born-again movement. We have noticed that, while there has been some reduction of the effect of the TV "black magicians," more and more individuals of the dark-hate groups of Christianity have taken it upon themselves to do the Lord's work by individually going on guerrilla raids against those who do not believe in their obsessions.

Although a full discussion is beyond the scope of this book, Mr. Black has been under continuous attack by a group of BAC (Born-Again Christians) who live next to his residence. The attack has taken the form of physical threats as well as calls to the police accusing him of being a "baby killer." The police have done nothing to protect Mr. Black; however, his magical counter-attacks against these groups have been successful, although extremely draining. Details of this insane attack on Mr. Black and me will appear in another work some time in 1998. We have both noticed that more and more individuals of the BAC are seizing the excuse of "The Millennium" to justify one-on-one violence against individuals in their personal environment. This is partly due to panic about the coming millennium and partly due to their loss of power in Washington, "BC".

Mr. Black has taken the trouble to monitor programs by the fundamentalists both on television and radio. In these "mediums" Satanic human sacrifice is asserted as an ongoing fact in spite of FBI conclusions to the contrary. Many of these organizations and churches distribute videos to their constituency on such subjects as the occult that can only be compared to Hitler's notorious *Eternal Jew* propaganda film. These objects are loaned out free to any churchgoers who feel they have "sinister neighbors."

This was done to Mr. Black—as well as illegal entry and search of his home (no, *not* by the police) and at least three other felonies. When these cowards realized to their astonishment that *they* were the criminals they committed yet another felony by conspiring to conceal evidence.

So much for Christian morality. We, of course, hold our morality to *The Book of the Law*. This, for those of you not familiar with Crowley, suggests non-interference with another's life unless it conflicts with yours in some *real* way—not violence in the name of Christian fantasy. In addition, *The Book of the Law* doesn't advocate initiatory violence but simple self protection.

You judge which is the more civilized.

Interestingly, at this same time, an increase in openly "diabolical" systems of practice has occurred in Europe and even in the United States. Popular media, both in the form of fiction and non-fiction, abounds with serious treatments of magic, as well as psychic and open attacks on fundamentalism and "Christendom" itself. This may partly explain the increasing agitation and paranoia that this segment of the population feels—Jimmy Swaggart once declared Science Fiction to be "satanic"—and their increased propensity to personal violence.

On the bright side, it shows an increasing tendency toward change away from the dark age, even if America goes through another inquisition on the way. Dr. Israel Regardie believed that this would be the case in the United States.

As a final word, remember the reasons why the old mages kept their activities secret. Those reasons are still valid. Take pains to make yourself safe in your surroundings and, above all, know the law and be able to present proof (in the form of video or audio tape) if what happened to us and others threatens to happen to you.

THE *Original* FALCON PRESS

Invites You to Visit Our Website:
http://originalfalcon.com

At our website you can:

- Browse the online catalog of all of our great titles
- Find out what's available and what's out of stock
- Get special discounts
- Order our titles through our secure online server
- Find products not available anywhere else including:
    - One of a kind and limited availability products
    - Special packages
    - Special pricing
- Get free gifts
- Join our email list for advance notice of New Releases and Special Offers
- Find out about book signings and author events
- Send email to our authors
- Read excerpts of many of our titles
- Find links to our authors' websites
- Discover links to other weird and wonderful sites
- And much, much more

Get online today at http://originalfalcon.com

Printed in Great Britain
by Amazon

23330944R00169